THE ESSENTIAL GUIDE TO
THE TAROT

XVIII – The Moon

THE ESSENTIAL GUIDE TO
THE TAROT

Understanding the Major and Minor Arcana

Using the Tarot to Find Self-knowledge and Change Your Destiny

DAVID FONTANA

WATKINS PUBLISHING
LONDON

The Essential Guide to the Tarot

David Fontana

First published in the United Kingdom
and Ireland in 2011 by
Watkins Publishing, an imprint of
Duncan Baird Publishers Ltd
Sixth Floor, Castle House
75–76 Wells Street
London W1T 3QH

Conceived, created and designed by
Duncan Baird Publishers

Managing Editor: Sandra Rigby
Editors: Jo Godfrey Wood, Fiona Robertson
Managing Designer: Suzanne Tuhrim
Commissioned artwork: Sylvie Daigneault

British Library Cataloguing-in-Publication Data:
A CIP record for this book is available from the
British Library

ISBN: 978-1-907486-83-8

10 9 8 7 6 5 4 3 2 1

Typeset in Adobe Garamond and Truesdell
Colour reproduction by Scanhouse, Malaysia
Printed in China by Imago

Publisher's note: Watkins Publishing, or any
other persons who have been involved in working
on this publication, cannot accept responsibility
for any injuries or damage incurred as a result of
following the information contained in this book.

Notes
Abbreviations used throughout this book:
CE Common Era (the equivalent of AD)
BCE Before the Common Era (the equivalent of BC)

Contents

XI – Justice

XVI – The Tower

Eight of Wands

Contents

Seven *of* Cups

One *of* Swords

Queen *of* Pentacles

Foreword

Many of us, blessed with an active imagination, are likely to have been intrigued by Tarot cards and want to know more about them. Where do they come from? What are they for? What do they mean? Anyone who knows the Tarot is likely to give different answers to these questions, for one of its virtues is its enigmatic nature. This is not a textbook full of clear and dogmatic answers. It is not a map with routes carefully marked. Above all, it is not a game for idle leisure or for gambling.

The Tarot, in its present form, is a tool for self-exploration and self-development – a tool to help the user to reflect upon the self and on life and its meaning. It is also a companion who can become helpful and wise, but never intrusive – a friend to hint, prompt and suggest rather than to lay down the law. As with all good friends, you can meet with the Tarot again and again, and it will always offer a welcome, always be ready to stimulate and inspire.

This book is an introduction for those who are new to the cards and a guide for those who are familiar with them but have no experience of their relevance for psychological and spiritual work. As well as giving some background to the cards and their history, it discusses their symbolism, their archetypal associations, their links with occult systems such as the Tree of Life and their use for inner development. It also covers their use for so-called Tarot readings, although it must be emphasized that this is by no means the only purpose of the cards. In particular, it explores each of the cards of the Major and the Minor Arcana (the two seemingly separate sections into which the deck is divided), indicating the meaning and purpose of each and explaining how they link together to form stages on a journey toward wisdom and understanding.

The idea of making a journey through a deck of cards may seem strange, but life itself, as we know, is a journey – from youth to old age, from birth to death. En route our steps pass through the emotional territory of our relationships with ourselves and with others; through the swings and hazards of circumstance; through the effort of acquiring and applying knowledge; and through the search for meaning and purpose in existence. We move toward a distant destination, where reality becomes clearer and we recognize our own truth as spiritual and physical beings. The Tarot can help us on our way.

Like all journeys, this one may lead, at times, to apparent dead-ends, to unwanted diversions, even to places where we have to go back and look again at scenery we passed earlier. But it takes us, ultimately, in the right direction; and it never punishes us for any wrong turnings. Like life itself, all the Tarot asks is a little commitment and perseverance, and the confidence to travel hopefully. I hope you enjoy the journey and find what you are seeking.

How to Use This Book

This is a book for all who wish to use the Tarot as a tool for self-discovery and self-development.

As a psychologist inspired by the work of that great intellectual pioneer Carl Jung, I have to admit that my own primary interest is in the inner journey adumbrated, in sequence, by the cards of the Major Arcana. On pages 48–137 I explain how you can trace this journey for yourself, arriving at unique insights into your own character, your own responses to the world, and your own deepest aspirations for yourself – your destiny, in other words.

Many people who use this book, however, are likely to wish to perform Tarot *readings*, based on "accidental" layouts of the cards. I placed that word in inverted commas because so many Tarot readers believe that the dealing of a particular layout, after shuffling the deck, is far from accidental. Chance, in their view, is guided by the operation of some kind of paranormal energy. At a simplistic level, this allows us to accept that a Tarot reading can be a clairvoyant glimpse of an individual's future – a fortune-telling. More profoundly, and more plausibly, there could be energies at work that emanate from a hidden spring of self-understanding, revealing our inner self to our outer apprehension.

It is easy to imagine someone approaching the Tarot for the first time being torn by conflicting impulses. On the one hand, they might well be attracted by the traditional, multi-layered symbolism. They might intuitively understand that symbols like the Hierophant and the World can serve as keys to aspects of our unconscious minds. At the same time, they might be sceptical about the paranormal dimension. The idea of "energies" might be too vague for them to accept.

Such a person need not be deterred from Tarot readings, because even if a layout results from pure chance, that is no reason to dismiss it as pointless. A chance configuration of cards can be revealing, not in what that particular pattern of symbols tells us, but in what we make of the pattern when we interpret its meaning for ourselves. This is the principle of the Rorschach ink test. Nobody would claim that the random ink blots are shaped by paranormal energies: the splodges are purely accidental, yet our response to them is not accidental at all, but derives from our psychological make-up.

In this book you will find my own interpretation of Tarot symbolism, which is less esoteric than some. By all means read the more mystical commentaries of, for example, A.E. Waite, whose own deck has proved so popular. Reflect on any aspect of the symbolism that you discover in books on the subject, or work out for yourself. Each person discovers and, in a sense, devises their own particular Tarot. Approach the cards with an open mind and a free imagination, trust in their complex profundity and your own interpretative style will evolve.

Introducing the Tarot

The Tarot is made up of two distinct parts. There are the Major Arcana, comprising 22 richly symbolic and highly individualized cards, including such familiar figures as the Fool and the Hanged Man; and there are the Minor Arcana, consisting of 56 cards which are divided into four suits – namely, wands, cups, swords and pentacles. Within each suit are pip cards that depict the numbers from one to ten, as well as four court cards – Princess, Prince, Queen and King.

For more than five hundred years, Tarot cards have intrigued, puzzled and inspired us, yet some of their secrets are still to be discovered. There is a tendency among some psychologists to dismiss the Tarot as no more than a set of vivid images into which people can read whatever meanings they like. Its use for so-called fortune-telling has contributed further to this dismissive scientific attitude. However, both psychologists and lay people who take the time to study and work with the Tarot

o – The **Fool**

recognize it as providing a unique set of archetypal symbols that can help us to access deep levels of the unconscious. Using the cards we can embark upon an exciting journey of self-discovery and self-development that takes in intellectual, emotional and spiritual aspects of our being. As with all journeys of self-discovery, there are no dogmatic rules about how to proceed. Human beings are infinitely complex and each person is very much an individual, so a great deal depends upon personal choice and reaction. What feels right for one may not feel right for another. However, as we shall see, there are sets of guidelines that have proved highly effective in revealing the underlying structure of our inner life. It is likely that the unknown authors (no doubt both male and female), who devised the cards, had an awareness of this structure based on their own intuition and psychological and spiritual experience.

My own interest in the Tarot goes back to my student days, when as an undergraduate I came across a reference to "a wicked pack of cards" in T.S. Eliot's poem *The Waste Land*, followed by enigmatic allusions to some of the individual cards that made up the deck. In Eliot's notes about the poem, he named this deck as the Tarot, and although I later found that some of his information about the cards was incorrect, the impression made upon me was that the Tarot has something important to teach us about the human psyche. At that

One of Swords

Subsequently, as a psychologist with a particular leaning toward the work of Jung and Freud and their emphasis upon the power of symbols and metaphors to open doors into the mysteries of the unconscious, I recognized how mistaken science has been to ignore the psychological relevance of the profound symbol systems – the ones that feature in the world's great religions and in esoteric practices such as alchemy and, of course, the Tarot.

These symbol systems are the product of minds acutely aware of the innate psychological forces that help to shape our thoughts and behaviour. As such, they serve not only as a way of revealing the secrets of these forces, but also as pathways to self-understanding and

time there was very little reliable literature available on the cards, and it was some years before I was even able to find and purchase a deck of my own. But I never lost my interest in the history and meaning of the cards, and in the relevance they might have for human psychology.

as tools for psychological and spiritual development.

One of our most pressing needs as human beings is to find meaning and purpose in life. Humankind is, in Jung's words, "as far as we know the only creature that can discover meaning". Without it, life is no more than a random biological machine: we may seek happiness in material pleasures, in possessions, in social status and in countless diversions of mind and body, and yet remain curiously unfulfilled. There is always a sense that there must be more to life than passing the time as pleasurably as possible, and that just beyond the horizon there is something more important and ultimately more satisfying, which all too often we fail to find. Modern research into happiness

shows that the most affluent communities are far from being the most contented: impoverished societies may score higher on this scale. If nothing else, we can conclude that happiness does not lie purely in material things.

As the great religious and spiritual traditions have long

Two of Pentacles

taught, we need instead to look to a spiritual dimension for our fulfilment – to a deeper level of our being that contains the true secret of our identity. This search brings us back to the Tarot. The cards are not part of any religion, nor are they in any sense a substitute for religion. They are essentially an aid toward an understanding of the energies within us that make us who we are.

This highly sophisticated tool arose by a complex evolution. The Minor Arcana may actually pre-date the Major Arcana. Some experts trace the Minor Arcana's origin to ancient China, while others believe that these pip and court cards may have originated in India and spread along the trade routes to Persia, Egypt and then Europe, where they were further popularized by soldiers who used the cards for gambling.

By the 13th century the Mamelukes in Egypt were using a pack with four suits – swords, polo sticks, cups and coins – that closely resembled the suits of the Minor Arcana. As the cards became more

Seven of Cups

widely available, many variations occurred, particularly among the court cards, which, with the exception of French decks, often featured a king and two marshals, omitting the queen.

One theory is that the Major Arcana were brought to Europe by fortune-telling gypsies, although an alternative idea is that these cards were simply invented as a set of trumps to supplement the games played with the Minor Arcana. If the latter theory is correct, the cards may, in fact, have originally had no particular symbolic meaning. However, their very nature strongly suggests that this is not the case: most probably their images were drawn from existing mystical symbol systems. Reflecting as they do profound archetypal

Eight of Wands

themes, the images are unlikely to have been chosen arbitrarily, and several attempts have been made to link them with the Knights Templar or with the Kabbalists or Alchemists. Although none of these attempts is entirely convincing, one thing is clear: the unknown authors knew exactly what they were doing.

Historic Decks

In 1392 the accounts of the Treasurer of the French King, Charles VI, record the purchase of three Tarot decks, and it is possible that 17 cards now in the collection of the Bibliothèque Nationale de France in Paris are from one of these. However, the Major Arcana did not make their earliest undisputed appearance until 1415, when a deck was hand-painted in Italy for the Duke of Milan. Later, hand-painted decks created for noble families appeared frequently in Italy and France.

The first printed decks appeared in Stuttgart (Germany) in 1440. The invention of woodblock printing enabled decks to proliferate, and despite the opposition of the Church (which associated the cards with the devil and saw them as a temptation to idle hands), the Tarot became increasingly popular.

Although many early Tarot decks included both Major and Minor Arcana, one deck of the 15th century, the Florentine Minchiate, shows the eclectic way in which the cards were sometimes treated at this period. This deck, used for a specific card game, includes not only the two Arcana but also cards for the zodiac signs, the four elements and the virtues Prudence, Faith, Hope and Charity.

Some subsequent decks replaced certain cards with secular alternatives in deference to the Church: the Pope became the Hierophant, the Papess the High Priestess. Sometimes the court cards depicted reigning monarchs.

From the outset, the Tarot was put to many different uses. Some churchmen used the cards to help the illiterate to remember Church doctrine, while at the popular level they were used for gaming and divination. At some point they also became associated with occult practices such as spells, and with the development of psychic powers.

Three decks were created in the mid-1600s for members of the Italian Visconti family, the most famous being the Visconti-Sforza deck, which was highly influential. Although the Tarot was soon to die out in northern Italy, it became well established in France and Switzerland. The Tarot de Marseille, which was introduced in the 18th century, was a landmark deck that set the parameters for many Tarots of the 19th century and beyond.

The Hermetic Order of the Golden Dawn, founded in London in 1888, saw the Tarot as a path to inner development. In the five years of its existence, the Golden Dawn had a major influence on esoteric thought and practice in Western Europe. Initiates in the Order were required to design and paint their own Tarot deck. One of these decks, by A.E. Waite, a leading member of the Order, was published by Rider and Co. in 1909, and has inspired many later designs. Waite recognized that the images and organization of the Tarot de Marseille represent key stages of spiritual self-discovery, and in so doing he came closest to the real purpose of the cards.

Modern Decks

When working with the Tarot it is important to find a deck that has both immediate and lasting appeal for you. There are at least 50 different Tarot decks on the market, each with its own distinctive flavour and most of them emphasizing a particular theme – such as vampires, fairies, witches and cats. Many such decks are commercial artefacts that deliberately move away from traditional imagery toward associations that a modern reader might see as being more contemporary and therefore more easily understandable.

However, there are various 20th-century decks that are rooted in traditional symbolism or reflect the world-view of genuine mystical or psychological seekers. Among these are Aleister Crowley's Thoth Tarot – Thoth being an ancient Egyptian deity. This deck, which was published posthumously in 1969, shows the Kings as mounted Knights (possibly for the sake of greater virility or dynamism) and renames a number of the Major Arcana – for example, Magician becomes Magus, Justice becomes Adjustment, Strength becomes Lust, Justice becomes Aeon and World becomes Universe. The imagery is permeated with ancient Egyptian, astrological and Kabbalistic associations.

Whereas the Tarot de Marseille is the most popular deck in Latin countries, the most successful deck in the English-speaking world generally is the Rider-Waite (see page 19). Created by the mystic

A.E. Waite and the illustrator Pamela Coleman Smith (both Golden Dawn members), the deck derives some of its symbolism from the 19th-century occultist Eliphas Levy. One distinctive feature of the design is the use of pictorial pip cards, which adds symbolic complexity to the Minor Arcana.

The cards used to illustrate the book you are reading now are from The Truth-Seeker's Tarot, devised by the author (see "Further Reading", page 280, for publication details). They have been designed with close attention to traditional Tarot symbolism: anyone who wishes to know how a particular card of the Major Arcana differs from its equivalent in, for example, the Tarot de Marseille or the Rider-Waite deck may consult the "Variations" sections in the card-by-card analysis that follows. In designing the Truth-Seeker's Tarot, we kept in mind the fact that the Tarot is a work of art, and that if it is to achieve its purpose, it must engage the senses artistically as well as appeal to the emotions, the intellect and the spirit.

King of Pentacles

Symbols

Although we may not be aware of the fact, symbols are a vital part of our lives. The impoverished cousin of the symbol is the sign – an example would be an outline of a man digging, indicating road works. Next on the scale comes the emblem, a picture that denotes specific qualities – a bank might opt for a castle as its logo to make us think of security. Finally comes the more complex individual image: the symbol, which seeks to represent universal truths difficult to express in words. Symbols tend to form without deliberate intention, as if part of our evolution as a species. Many are found across cultures right through the centuries. Rooted within our own unconscious minds, they serve as keys to these often inaccessible parts of ourselves, and thus can help us to reach new levels of self-understanding – which in turn is a good basis for self-development.

Symbols can take the form of devices such as the cross, the circle, the square and the triangle, or of concepts that have deep emotional resonance, such as mother and

XVIII – The **Moon**

father, hero and monster, God and soul. Or they can be images of natural phenomena, such as the sun, the moon, the lion, the butterfly; or products of the imagination, such as the dragon.

Symbols can move and inspire us, revealing our hopes, fears and aspirations. Through them we access deeper aspects of our own being – levels of intuitive wisdom that we hardly knew existed. In helping us to realize our inner potential, they tell us more about who we really are.

The great religions and spiritual traditions of the world have always made extensive use of symbols, allowing the faithful to draw closer to sacred truths. Magical and occult fraternities, such as the Rosicrucians, the Freemasons and

King of Swords

the Order of the Golden Dawn, have relied heavily on symbols to convey ideas that are integral to their belief systems. Much of the symbolism used by such people has roots in the hermetic and alchemical traditions, whose distant origins lie in ancient Egypt and medieval Europe.

XI – **Justice**

For many centuries symbols have offered a vivid, instantly accessible lexicon of belief that has been central in the lives not only of priests, shamans and storytellers, but also of the common people. Imagine for a moment the importance that animals, such as the coyote and eagle, have had in the world-view of Native tribes; or plants such as the mistletoe and the oak in the Celtic druidic tradition.

Symbols are particularly potent, of course, in the pre-literate civilizations, yet their significance goes far beyond the obvious one of instructing and inspiring. They also have a power that takes us into the realm of the paranormal, since they can equip us to contact and perhaps control the forces of nature and the unseen worlds of the spirits and the ancestors.

Western scientific psychology (with the exceptions of psychoanalytical and analytical psychology and, more recently, transpersonal psychology) has tended to underestimate the importance of symbols. However, the creative arts have long focused on symbolism, which enables readers to see far more in a poem, audiences to see far more in a play, observers to see far more in a painting than is actually shown. A symbol is a portable mirror that reflects a complex whole. Symbols touch and arouse the emotions, enabling an intimate form of identification to take place between the creative artist and the public, and confirming the nature and extent of our shared humanity.

Symbols are also widely used as a focus of attention in meditation. The meditator gazes at the symbol while the mind remains open and uncluttered by thoughts; then, with eyes closed, he or she holds the symbol in the visual imagination. If the image begins to fade, the meditator opens the eyes again and attempts to visualize the image again. Used in this way, the symbol speaks directly to the unconscious, arousing insights into its deeper levels of meaning – both during the meditation and in the days that follow. Typically, the meditator chooses symbols associated with his or her belief system, and often finds that one or other symbol arises as a favourite, conveying personal meanings and stimulating profound levels of awareness. From the Tarot, one of the cards of the Major Arcana is usually chosen. For example, the Tower, which shows the destruction of pride or the release of repressed feelings, might inspire us to achieve in our lives the sense of liberation and fresh beginnings that resonates in this imagery.

Archetypes

Both Sigmund Freud (1856–1939), the founder of psychoanalysis, and the analytical psychologist Carl Jung (1875–1961) emphasized the importance of symbols in our inner lives. In their work with neurotic and disturbed patients, they recognized a universal symbolic language that reveals itself in dreams and in our deepest imaginings (for example, in free association). Exploring this language, they found that they were able to go deeper into the unconscious minds of their patients and uncover long-forgotten early memories that gave clues as to the causes of deep-rooted problems. For Freud many of these memories were associated with repressed sexual desires, and he considered that many frequently occurring symbols, especially in our dream worlds, carry strong sexual meaning. Jung, who largely rejected this emphasis on sexuality, saw symbols as having a far wider relevance for our psychological lives, representing the major themes of human existence, such as life and death, male and female, loss and redemption, and our search for deeper truths. Jung used the term "archetype" to represent these and other key themes and the symbols that best represent them.

Archetypal symbols play a central role in the Tarot cards, particularly in the Major Arcana. These symbols make the cards potentially effective in analytical and other, similar psychotherapies. The psychotherapist may, for example, invite the client to

JUNGIAN CORRESPONDENCES

	CARD	ARCHETYPE
0	The Fool	The Wanderer
i	The Magician	The Trickster
ii	The High Priestess	The Virgin
iii	The Empress	The Mother
iv	The Emperor	The Father; the Hero
v	The Hierophant	The Wise Old Man
vi	The Lovers	The Soul
vii	The Chariot	The Persona
viii	Strength	–
ix	The Hermit	The Wise Old Man
x	The Wheel of Fortune	–
xi	Justice	–
xii	The Hanged Man	–
xiii	Death	Rebirth
xiv	Temperance	The union of opposites as defined in Jung's *Mysterium Coniunctionis*
xv	The Devil	–
xvi	The Tower	Chaos
xvii	The Star	The Star
xviii	The Moon	The Anima
xix	The Sun	The Animus
xx	Judgment	–
xxi	The World	–

The Tarot includes a number of the primary archetypes that were highlighted by Jung for their importance in "individuation" (the process of psychological self-development), among them being the Anima and the Animus, and the Wise Old Man. Other psychologically signficant archetypes of transformation, such as the Hero, the Mother and the Star, may also be linked with the Major Arcana. The table here lists approximate correspondences where these can be clearly identified. A dash means that no obvious equivalent suggests itself.

construct narratives around selected cards, in the hope that these stories will yield insights into the client's anxieties, hopes and aspirations. In spinning his tales, the client may then unconsciously project onto the cards complexes, repressed memories or hidden desires. This way of working is akin to that of Jungian dream analysis. It also resembles, in some ways, the Rorschach test used by some psychotherapists, in which the client interprets a series of ambiguous ink blots in the light of their preoccupations. However, the Tarot method goes much further, in that it uses archetypal images that are known to resonate directly with important areas of the unconscious. Of course, such voyages of self-discovery are not just for people seeking the help of psychotherapists. Well-adjusted people can also benefit hugely by using the Tarot cards in this way.

Jung argued that there are three levels in the unconscious mind. The first level, the pre-conscious, contains all the information that we can access at will. The second level, the personal unconscious, consists of our hidden memories, our repressed wishes, fears and hopes, our traumas, defence mechanisms, complexes and prejudices. Although the personal unconscious is, for much of the time, beyond the reach of our conscious mind, it is a major influence on our thinking and behaviour, and it is this level that the psychotherapist attempts to access. The third level is the so-called "collective unconscious", which Jung considered to be shared by the whole human race. Rather as we are born with a common biological blueprint that shapes our bodies, so Jung saw the collective unconscious as a form of shared psychological blueprint that shapes our mental and emotional lives. It also contains spiritual awareness, our sense of God, of life beyond death and of the meaning of our short stay upon this planet.

The archetypes are innate psychological and spiritual energies within the collective unconscious, symbolized for us in the form of human or other images. It is these characters that are portrayed in the Tarot. Since we all have the archetypes in our psychological make-up, we also have within us certain aspects of each Major Arcana card. For example, we have the Magician, who tries to weave spells and make things happen; we have the Emperor and Empress, who are our Father and Mother; we have the Hermit, who is our Wise Old Man; we have the Hanged Man, who is the victim yet triumphs over adversity; and we have Temperance, symbolizing restraint and sometimes union. It is a mistake to think of these symbols as being too clearly defined: there is always something equivocal about the archetypes. They represent strengths yet also weaknesses. They are flowing energies, not static presences. Working with them in the Tarot can help to reveal this to us and thus demonstrate our own ambivalent nature.

Divination

The desire to divine the future has been with humankind since the dawn of history and doubtless long before that. A whole variety of methods, ranging from gazing into pools of black ink or crystal balls to studying the entrails of animals or listening to entranced women ("oracles") have been used for this purpose.

Studying the lines on the palm of the hand, the position of the stars and the planets at birth, the pattern made by tea leaves at the bottom of a cup and even the behaviour of animals, have all been thought, at various times, to foretell the future; and so-called fortune tellers or psychics have always found ready listeners. Not surprisingly, modern playing cards and in particular Tarot cards,

popularized for fortune-telling by the Russian mystic and co-founder of the Theosophical Society Madame Blavatsky (1831–1891), are favourite tools of the diviner.

But can we really divine the future, as opposed to making informed guesses based on present circumstances? According to

X – The **Wheel** of **Fortune**

modern science, such an ability, known as precognition, cannot exist, although for more than 70 years parapsychological research has been producing evidence under controlled laboratory conditions that appears to suggest that on rare occasions the feat may be possible. This research simply looks at what seems to occur in the experiment, without attempting to advance explanations as to the cause. However, one popular theory claiming to explain how divination works is that nothing happens by chance. Thus, if we shuffle a deck of Major Arcana cards and lay them out in a pattern on the table, the order in which the cards occur is due not to chance but to some unseen process we do not yet understand. Carl Jung referred to this process as "acausal" – events or objects are brought together not through a connection of cause and effect but by virtue of a shared meaning of some kind. By studying the symbolism of each card and its relationship to the other cards in the arrangement, it is thought possible to trace a shared meaning between the pattern of the cards and an individual's destiny. This meaning is seen as the means not only to "read" someone's character strengths and weaknesses but also to divine what his or her future might hold.

Unfortunately, it appears that no conclusive scientific research has been carried out into theories of this nature. Laboratory work on precognition involves something much less complicated than an

THE SEVEN-CARD HORSESHOE LAYOUT

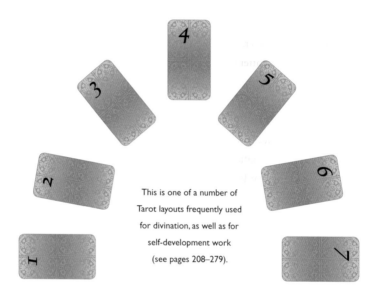

This is one of a number of Tarot layouts frequently used for divination, as well as for self-development work (see pages 208–279).

individual's future life, such as measuring if a person shows an unconscious "startle" response (which is measurable by sensitive physiological instruments) to the sight of unpleasant pictures, even before the computer has randomly selected these pictures for display from a set containing pleasant as well as unpleasant images.

To try to predict what is beyond our control – for example, our health, or whether we will have a grandson, and when, is more to do with superstition than with true destiny based on character. It is as well to remember that attempts to divine someone's future from Tarot cards or other aids, even if the intention is light-hearted, can be dangerous psychologically if they lead to significant expectations or anxieties. The Tarot is far better used for its real purpose – namely, helping people to look at where they are now rather than where they may or may not be in years to come. Decisions about the future will follow on naturally from this.

We usually think of divination as finding out about the future, but the term really means gaining knowledge of the unknown (as in, for example, water divining). And since the Tarot can help you toward self-knowledge, it is truly a form of

Prince of Swords

self-divination. Bear in mind too that "divination" comes from the same root as "divine", which brings to mind the idea of obtaining a more profound knowledge of the spiritual dimension of being; and this in turn reminds us that the Tarot is essentially a pathway to higher wisdom.

Self-development

The Tarot is a visual tool to help us on the journey toward greater self-understanding. Working through the cards in stages can enable us to develop our imagination, delve deeper within ourselves, and progress both psychologically and spiritually.

Stage 1

At the famous shrine of Apollo at Delphi in Greece there is an engraving that counsels, "Know Thyself." This might sound odd. Surely we know ourselves? Yet in Zen Buddhist training, students are also asked to ponder the question "Who am I?" The point is that although we think we know plenty about ourselves (our names, our occupations, our likes and dislikes, and some of our personal characteristics), these are only labels or, at best, descriptions. They fail to capture the mystery of our true identity. We are in touch with our conscious and pre-conscious minds, but the much vaster dimensions of our personal unconscious and of the collective unconscious remain hidden from us. It is as if we live in a gorgeous house but have never ventured into the vast inner rooms, even though it is the content of these rooms that determines much of who we are.

By familiarizing ourselves with this content we can come to understand ourselves, and the reasons why we are as we are, much better than before. Also, we can help ourselves to find answers to pressing questions about the meaning and purpose of our lives –

even attaining an answer to the searching conundrum of whether we are more than just brains and bodies that begin at birth and end at death. This process of self-exploration is referred to as "self-development". Setting ourselves on this path, we take more control over our lives and deal more effectively with our anxieties, at the same time lifting our spirits and growing in self-awareness, self-confidence and wisdom.

The Tarot can assist this process if we see it as a series of archetypal symbols that take us through the unexplored inner rooms. Some writers on the Tarot also see these symbols as conveying concepts about the nature of the universe, a view inspired by the Hermetic allegory (derived from ancient

Queen of Wands

Egyptian, Greek and early Christian writings) that claims, "As above, so below" – in other words, the idea that humankind, the microcosm, is a representation of the macrocosm, the greater reality that encompasses the universe and all it contains; and that by knowing more about ourselves we come to

o – The **Fool**

of ourselves. Why should we identify with the Fool? In fact, the Fool, as we shall see when we come to explore each of the cards, is not quite what he seems. His foolishness is not of the empty-headed kind. Instead, there are two aspects of his nature that require him to be taken seriously. First, he differs from his fellow men and women in being dissatisfied with the superficial things that please most people. In this sense we should perhaps call him an outsider rather than a fool. Secondly, he is foolish in his readiness to step into the unknown, to launch himself off the supposed safety of the cliff into thin air to embark on a journey that leads into the unknown. His foolishness is therefore a potential virtue, the foolishness of longing

know more of the eternal realities of creation itself. This allegory is best illustrated by the relationship between the Tarot archetypes and the pathways on the Kabbalistic Tree of Life (see pages 42–5).

In working with the Tarot, we always start with the Fool, the holy innocent, who is in fact an aspect for something beyond himself, of hope, of the courage to explore the mysterious, to aspire to wisdom and understanding, to sacrifice the mundane for the sublime. The Fool is the start of the journey of the Tarot.

Stage 2

To work with the Tarot we need to use the powers of imagination, in particular the visual imagination. Research in transpersonal psychology – the study of our deeper levels of inner experience, such as dreams, creativity, meditation, empathetic feelings and spiritual experiences – has shown that the imagination and the ability to visualize are effective aids to self-discovery and self-development, as well as to progress during psychotherapy and psychological counselling. The focused use of the imagination is not a form of idle daydreaming, but an effective tool not only for assisting physical and psychological healing but also for enhancing the ability of the conscious mind to contact the creative levels of the personal and even the collective unconscious. When the focus of visualization is an archetypal symbol, such as one of the Tarot cards, the practice becomes not only easier to do but more likely to produce results.

Each Tarot card has its own unique contribution to make, as we shall see, but it is best to concentrate initially upon the Major Arcana, working through the cards in their numerical order (as they appear in this book), spending sufficient time on each card for you to be able to visualize it clearly with eyes closed. Remember that time means nothing in work of this kind. You may spend days on each card, or even weeks. Some cards will prove easier for you than others. But never be tempted to try to hurry things. First, read in the following pages the description of the card you are working on, then place it somewhere where you can see it frequently, such as on a mantelpiece or a bookshelf. Glance at it or study it more closely each time you pass by. Close your eyes to see if you can retain the image. Visualize it before drifting off to sleep at night. Ask yourself what the card represents or suggests to you. Don't worry if this differs from the description of the card given in this or other books. It is what the card means to *you* that matters. Symbols work best if we do not try to be too analytical about them. Let the card appeal directly to your creative unconscious and note what emerges. Try drawing or painting the card if you like – one of the practices used by the Golden Dawn – as this often serves to fix the image in the mind or to inspire you to add details of your own. But as with any visualization exercise, discontinue the practice at any point, here or later in your work with the cards, if you find it becoming too intrusive or in any way disturbing. The card is there to help you, not to trouble you.

I – The Magician

Visualization requires practice. It comes easily to most artists, but for the rest of us practice is needed. We are all born with the ability, but like all abilities, if it isn't used, we lose it. Happily, improvement comes quickly, and once the skill develops, we can use it in other areas of life. The Tarot is especially effective as a means of training in visualization, not only because its colours and pictorial interest are attractive, but also because the archetypal symbols portrayed are already present in our unconscious and therefore familiar to our visual imagination.

Stage 3

Start your visualization work with Card I, the Magician. Once you can visualize the Magician with your eyes closed and are able to hold the image without effort, imagine that he is in a picture you are looking at. Then put a frame around the picture (ask your imagination to create the frame: it will do so spontaneously, often with interesting results). Once the picture within its frame is clear to you, step in your imagination through the frame and into the image. Don't try too hard or expect the scene to be too realistic. Just step through into the scene and see what happens. Allow events to unfold around you as they do in dreams. See the Magician in front of you, with scenery behind and to the sides of him, as depicted in the card. Essentially, you are doing no more than an artist is doing when, in imagination, he or she becomes part of the picture being painted, or than a novelist does when a character starts coming to life – or than your own dreaming mind does for you in sleep.

When you have taken in the scene, step backward out of the frame and close the visualization by letting it fade from your mind and telling yourself that you are now back in the present. The ability to close the visualization is part of the exercise. If you find any difficulty in doing this, it's better to discontinue your visualization work, at least for now, and simply work with the cards as abstract ideas. Do not try to hang on to the scene, to store it in your mind, otherwise you will lose the sense of freshness and immediacy the next time you do the visualization exercise, with the result that your experience will become artificial and ultimately meaningless.

Afterwards ask yourself what the experience has conveyed to you. You stepped into the picture in the role of the Fool and met the Magician. How did you relate to him? Did he communicate with you in any way? Did you enjoy his company? What were your feelings about him? Don't worry if this exercise proved difficult or if you saw nothing inside the picture, or the Magician didn't come to imaginary life. Next time things may be different, but it doesn't matter whether they are or not. Effects don't have to be dramatic with the Tarot. The symbols work in their own way for each person.

III – The **Empress**

More details will be given as we go through the cards, but the above example provides the basic practice for use with all the cards, each of which takes you deeper into your journey. With experience you may introduce your own variations, but the principles behind this practice have not only been developed through long use by Tarot adepts, but also feature in the guided visualization sessions used by many transpersonal psychotherapists. The secret is to allow the unconscious to do the work for you – and never persist with any practices designed to explore the unconscious if they cause you to feel alarm or anxiety of any kind.

The Tree of Life

The Tarot is a self-contained and well-established system within the Western tradition, and one that is perfectly able to function on its own, without reference to other systems of esoteric thought. As Jung pointed out in another context, in psychological and spiritual work it is generally preferable for people to work within their own cultural tradition, which has evolved in response to specific social and historical circumstances. However, there is much fascination to be derived from parallels that can be traced between the Tarot and the Kabbalistic Tree of Life – an important symbol of Jewish mysticism. The Order of the Golden Dawn devoted a great deal of intellectual energy to this topic.

The Tree of Life, or Sephiroth (singular: Sephirah), is a symbol comprising ten circles or spheres joined together by 22 crisscrossing pathways. The image reflects the relationships between various sets of occult symbols – for example, the Hebrew alphabet (whose letters have esoteric significance), the numbers from one to ten and their meanings, the zodiac signs and the planets of astrology – as well as the cards of the Tarot.

Western magic since the Golden Dawn has used a version of the Tree that can be traced back at least as far as Athanasius Kircher's *Oedipus Aegyptiacus*, published in 1652. Each of the 22 pathways relates to one of the Major Arcana of the Tarot, while the Sephiroth themselves are related to the pip

THE SEPHIROTH

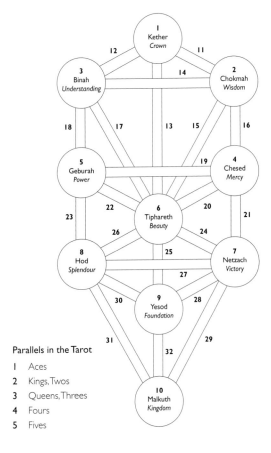

6   Princes, Sixes

7   Sevens

8   Eights

9   Nines

10   Princesses, Tens

11   The Fool

12   The Magician

13   The High Priestess

14   The Empress

15   The Emperor

16   The Hierophant

17   The Lovers

18   The Chariot

19   Strength

20   The Hermit

21   The Wheel of Fortune

22   Justice

23   The Hanged Man

24   Death

25   Temperance

26   The Devil

27   The Tower

28   The Star

29   The Moon

30   The Sun

31   Judgment

32   The World

Parallels in the Tarot

1   Aces

2   Kings, Twos

3   Queens, Threes

4   Fours

5   Fives

o – The **Fool**

cards and the court cards. To use the system arising from these correspondences you need a working knowledge of the principles associated with the Sephiroth, which have to do with the relationship between the Creator, the highest Sephirah (Kether or the Crown), and his creation (Malkuth, the Kingdom, the lowest Sephirah). This relationship is symbolized as passing downward through the pathways connecting the intermediate Sephiroth (Wisdom, Understanding, Mercy, Power, Beauty, Victory, Splendour and the Foundation) to Kether, Malkuth and each other. An ancient occult practice adopted by the Golden Dawn, known as "Rising on the Planes", involves passing through each of the Sephiroth in turn, until the adept finally approaches the ultimate reality of Kether. In this practice the appropriate Tarot card is used to provide a focus for meditation at each stage.

Other occult systems have linked the Sephiroth and thus the Tarot cards with the chakras – the

XXI – The **World**

non-physical energy and consciousness centres of the body. The chakras are claimed in yoga philosophy to concentrate and transform the distribution of physical energy throughout the body and also to channel the ascent of this energy up through the body until it is transmuted into spiritual energy at the Sahasrara, the highest chakra, situated just above the crown of the head. You can, for example, replace the Sanskrit symbols for each of the seven chakras with three cards from the Major Arcana, so using all 21 cards (excluding the Fool, who actually makes the ascent), visualizing each of the three cards in turn as the physical, mental and spiritual aspect of a particular chakra. When the sense of the movement of energy from physical to spiritual is firmly established for a chakra, you can then move on to the next level.

All the occult systems associated, however tenuously, with the Tarot cards depend upon visualizing a progression of Tarot images culminating in the final card, Card XXI, the World.

The Major Arcana

One way of thinking about the Tarot is that the Major Arcana represent the inner world of mind and spirit, and the Minor Arcana the outer world of body and the physical environment. Seen in this way, both parts of the Tarot have their specific roles to play in illuminating our understanding of reality. Most people find more fascination in the Major Arcana on account of their rich archetypal symbolism. As the inner world is where we live, the Major Arcana are the best starting-point for our work on the Tarot.

Introduction

The Major Arcana (meaning "Major Mysteries" or "Major Secrets", from the Latin *arcere*, "to enclose") are the part of the Tarot that contains more archetypal symbols, and carries the deeper levels of meaning. These symbols represent the unseen yet vitally important dimension that we experience, all through our waking and dreaming lives, as the essence of ourselves.

The 22 cards of the Major Arcana are arranged in numerical order from the Fool (0) to the World (XXI), although in some decks the Fool, still numbered 0, is placed at the end. Using the deck sequentially, rather than reading a layout such as the Horseshoe or Celtic Cross, it is important to work through the cards in numerical order, as this represents progressive stages on the journey of self-exploration. You may spend longer on some cards than others, as their deeper meaning and relevance are more slowly revealed. The nature of this journey will become clear as we deal with each card in the following pages.

The quest commences with the first step taken by the Fool, carefree and unaware of the mysteries ahead. Assuming that the material world is all that exists, he knows little of the non-physical dimension. He is portrayed as a fool because he is not yet aware of who he really is – that is, an eternal spirit incarnated within a mortal body. Even so, he is conscious of elusive hints and whispers from deep within himself that suggest that there may be more to life than the physical. It is these hints that prompt him to set out on his journey.

On this quest the Fool will meet symbolic aspects of his own true mental and spiritual self, personified as a series of mysterious men and women. Each is there to help him, although he must come to know them better before the nature of this help becomes clear. Some of the people he meets, although intrinsically good, have a darker side which, like human nature itself, can deceive and lead astray. Even the highest qualities and motives can become destructive. Kindness can become insincerity, responsibility can turn into authoritarianism, knowledge can become dogma, love can lead to jealousy. The Fool has to learn the differences between these extremes, and how to seek the one and reject the other.

Card XXI, the World, is the journey's end. The Fool will only know its true nature when he arrives – and may find, when he does, that the end of his quest is in fact a fresh beginning.

X – The Wheel of Fortune

0 – The *Fool*

Carrying his worldly possessions, the baggage of his old self, the Fool sets out on his journey, poised between the illusory stability of the physical world behind and the expansive unknown of the spiritual dimension ahead. He has the support of his staff (his innate good sense), and is accompanied by his pet dog (his instincts), who tries to warn him of the perils that may await. In identifying with the Fool, we must be aware not only of his foolishness but also of his strengths. He has not chosen to follow the easier paths of the physical world. Instead he sets out hopefully, led by the vague impression that there must be something beyond the transitory nature of his former life. He is also equipped with imagination, fundamental goodness and a wish to find purpose and meaning.

In meditating on the Fool it can be helpful to think about where you are in your life right now. We all have some of the Fool's innocence and some of his hopefulness, and it is good to try to recognize these qualities in yourself. Where do you hope the journey will lead? What do you want from the Tarot? It must be something beyond the hard facts. No two travellers will ever end up in the same place. In your journeying, try to remember that the Tarot is also about appreciating life to the full. The road is best travelled with a light, enquiring spirit. It is about wisdom, not confusion; joy, not anxiety.

0 – The *Fool*

Keywords

Illusion

Hope

The Unknown

Perils

Innocence

Strengths

Imagination

Enjoyment

Wisdom

The Fool: in detail

Blue skies: The Fool sets out under blue skies – symbol of joy and optimism. The small clouds hint at possible future changes in the weather. The Fool, however, looking elsewhere, fails to see them.

Jester's cap: This was not a sign of disgrace in medieval times, as it is today. The Fool was valued at Court: his foolishness was often seen as wiser than the supposed good sense of those around him.

Shoulder bag: A container of worldly goods and thus of the Fool's old self. This prompts us to ask: How much unnecessary baggage do we carry with us in life?

Cliff edge: This suggests uncertainty and possible danger. Should the Fool stay on firm ground or should he make the leap of faith?

Dog: The little dog symbolizes our instincts, which are sometimes helpful, sometimes a hindrance. The Fool is aware of the dog's efforts to warn him, but he chooses to keep going forward nonetheless.

Variations

- The early Visconti-Sforza Fool (*c.*1450) has no dog and is standing, not walking. He is dressed in rags and has feathers in his hair, and is more mendicant than entertainer.

*o – The **Fool***

- The image of the Fool with his jester's cap, his shoulder bag and a dog worrying at his leg goes back to at least 1500.

- The Marseille version shows a bearded Fool – suggesting that even those with plenty of life experience have much to learn.

- The clifftop first appeared in the Rider-Waite deck, with mountains beyond. This Fool swaggers proudly. The sky has the sun, rather than clouds – perhaps suggesting self-delusion (mountain weather can quickly turn bad).

- The Golden Dawn Tarot depicts a naked child plucking a yellow rose from a tree, and holding a grey wolf on a leash.

Starting-points

- Ignorance of one's true self
- There is more to life than the material world
- The search for meaning
- Possible hazards on the traveller's path
- Determination and courage
- Foolishness and wisdom

I – The *Magician*

The Magician is often selected by people as their favourite Tarot card, perhaps because he represents mystery and power. But his power is enigmatic. There is something of the travelling showman about him, a mysterious stranger who captures the attention of simple townsfolk by sleight of hand as well as real magic. He guards entry to the Major Arcana and reminds us of the illusory nature of the material world and that our view of reality may have to change if we are to proceed further. The table is levitating, but is this genuine magic? He leaves it to the Fool to decide, and to recognize how easily the mind is deceived by appearances. The Magician's number is one, the number of creation and new beginnings; the brim of his hat forms the number eight, symbol of infinity and the eternal cycle of life.

On the table are the four symbols used in the Minor Arcana (wand, sword, pentacle, cup) and his right hand performs a magic pass over them, as if he can make them appear or disappear – perhaps dependent upon the Fool's wishes. With the wand he points up to the sky, indicating the unity of heaven and earth.

The Magician challenges us to accept that things are not what they seem, that there is a deeper reality, and that truth is found by looking inward, into our own minds. Meditating on the Magician and the questions he poses on the nature of reality and illusion is a vital part of the Tarot.

Keywords

Magus

Illusion / Reality

Infinity

Transformation

Appearances

Mind

I – The *Magician*

The Magician: in detail

Objects: The Magician stands outside the world we take for granted. He lives by his own rules, can weave spells, and can make things appear and disappear. Everything in the material world is impermanent.

Hat: A hat is a symbol of secrecy and magic. The Magician's hat may make us wonder what he keeps underneath it. Perhaps he has more to teach us. The figure eight, without beginning or end, is the union of two spheres, heaven and earth. Earth is an illusory copy of heaven, lacking the truth and perfection of the original.

Table: The Magician's table floats in the air, defying gravity. Like the table we can free ourselves from the gravity that restricts our way of seeing. The miraculous can happen, often in small ways that we might not even notice.

Magic wand: What is our own transforming wand? We may decide that it is the power of the will. The Magician reminds us that our understanding may also be transformed if we are brave enough to adopt a new perspective on life.

Variations

- Starting as a mountebank, or showman, this figure evolved in time into the more ambiguous magician of the occult decks.

- Rider-Waite shows the Magician with one hand, holding the wand, pointing up to heaven; the other is pointing down to the ground. This emphasizes his role as an intermediary between worlds. The lilies and roses in this card suggest heavenly aspiration.

- Most decks emphasize the Magician's exceptional power – he is not like other men. Aleister Crowley renames him the "Magus", and shows him on winged feet reaching up to the heavens, reminding us that he is sometimes identified with Mercury.

- The Magician is one of the most variable images in the Major Arcana. Perhaps this demonstrates his shape-changing powers.

I – The *Magician*

Starting-points

- Alternative views of reality must always be considered
- Outsiders can transform our view of life
- The possibility of deception
- Creation and new beginnings
- The relationship of heaven to earth
- The magic of the mind

II – The *High Priestess*

It is logical that the High Priestess follows the Magician, for she is a card of initiation. The Fool has been initiated by the Magician into the transforming power of the Tarot, and now he can be initiated into a second, higher, level: the Tarot's spiritual power. The High Priestess also introduces him to the domain of the female, thus complementing the masculine domain of the Magician. In myths, the female domain is one of hidden mysteries. It is she who knows the path through the dark forest and leads the traveller from ignorance to wisdom, although often he fails to make proper use of her gift.

The High Priestess reminds us that spiritual progress depends upon accessing our female as well as our masculine side. We each possess both sides, and whereas the masculine is traditionally seen as concerned with visible things, with activity and the direct confrontation of ignorance, the female represents hidden and mysterious wisdom, the esoteric rather than the exoteric dimension. She is the moon compared to the sun, and in ancient traditions it was she who received messages from the spiritual worlds, which her masculine counterpart then interpreted and put into effect.

When working with the High Priestess we should ask ourselves whether we understand what is meant by the "feminine side", and whether we are open to the subtle mysteries that come from the unseen world to which this side of ourselves has access.

II – The *High Priestess*

Keywords

Mystic

Initiation

The Feminine

Intuition

Esoteric

Concealment

The High Priestess: in detail

Veil: Behind the High Priestess is a curtain – a thick veil. This hints at hidden things that she is not yet prepared to reveal. It separates our outer and inner worlds.

Blue: The blue of her robe symbolizes spirituality, calm and tranquillity. Behind her the curtain is purplish: the subtle shade of blue associated with mystical experience. Perhaps the drapes hide the most exalted secrets of all?

Book: The High Priestess holds a book, signifying learning and wisdom. The pages are partly concealed by her hand and her sleeve, implying that the book will be read only by those who are worthy of it. Its wisdom is not secret, but whether we can read it or not depends upon our will to do so, as well as our powers of understanding.

Throne: The High Priestess sits on a wooden throne. She has no wish to appear regal or to suggest that spirituality is always comfortable. The throne's crosspieces at either side of her head remind us, in fact, of Christ's cross, and of a life that rejected comfort and instead chose suffering.

Variations

• Early decks represent the High Priestess as a female Pope. The Visconti-Sforza shows her wearing a papal tiara and holding a closed book in one hand, a sceptre in the other. The Marseille deck's "Papesse" has a closed book in her lap. Some later decks, including Rider-Waite, show her wearing a cross as a pendant.

II – The **High Priestess**

• One variant of the Tarot de Marseille replaces the controversial female Pope – perhaps a reference to the legendary Pope Joan – with an image of the goddess Juno and her peacock.

• Rider-Waite has the High Priestess seated between a black pillar (with "B" on it) and a black pillar (with "J"). The pillars, symbolizing cosmic balance, are from Solomon's Temple and refer to Boaz (In Strength) and Jachin (He Establishes). The seated priestess has a crescent moon at her feet – on many decks there is a moon in her headdress.

Starting-points

- The importance of the feminine
- Relationship between exoteric and esoteric
- The possibility of seeing beyond the veil
- The importance of the will
- The reality of suffering

III – The Empress

Whereas the High Priestess represents the mysterious, spiritual side of the female, the Empress shows her complementary instinctive side: the Earth Mother, fertility, emotions, nurture, sustenance. Meeting her, the Fool examines his understanding of other people's feelings.

The High Priestess can be aloof, yet the Empress is warm. In contrast to the High Priestess' concern with wisdom and the unconscious, the Empress is concerned with feelings and consciousness, and the flourishing of creativity. Enthroned in nature's abundance, she urges the Fool to appreciate the wonders of the natural world, to be grateful for its generosity and to see nature as a miracle – the creation of being from non-being, the magical transformation of unseen spiritual potential into bountiful physical life. However, nature can be cruel: the warmth and light of summer can turn into a cold, dark winter. The Empress can become the over-possessive, demanding mother. We must remain a little wary of her, because she can distract us with her material gifts but can also remove these gifts at will.

Moving through the Tarot does not mean that the earlier cards are left behind. Their influence remains, modifying the traveller's relationship with later cards and reappearing when guidance is needed. Much is learned by placing the High Priestess and the Empress side by side and meditating on these two aspects of the female.

III – The *Empress*

Keywords

Fertility

Emotions

Consciousness

Creativity

Potential

Kindness / Possessiveness

Bounty

The Empress: in detail

Orb and cross: The two symbols that surmount the Empress' staff indicate her relationship to the physical world (the orb) and the spiritual world (the cross). Together they stand for the mystic union between spirit and matter, and male and female, that brings forth life and nature.

Crown: Symbol of the Empress' regal status, and also of the gifts given to us at birth, it contrasts with the less ostentatious coronet worn by the High Priestess, further emphasizing the difference between the women. The Empress leaves us in no doubt of her status; the High Priestess shows her humility.

Shield: Although the Empress has no weapons, she carries a shield – the power of nature to protect herself from mistakes made by humankind. Nature existed before we did and will exist long after we are gone. The mythic eagle symbolizes the sun, on which nature depends just as we depend on nature.

Trees: The summer offers us pleasing profusion, contrasting with the profusion of artifice – exemplified by the luxurious cuffs on the Empress' sleeves. A wood is a place in which to lose ourself and find ourself.

Variations

- As her meaning is unequivocal, the Empress shows little variation between decks. Regal symbols (the crown, the throne) often appear, as does the emphasis on the earth mother role.

- The Empress is typically seated, making eye contact with the observer, suggesting an unsubtle directness. The Aleister Crowley Thoth deck, however, depicts her in profile.

- In many decks the Empress' shield carries the image of an eagle – a sun symbol, emphasizing her difference from the High Priestess, whose heavenly body is the moon.

- Rider-Waite portrays the Empress wearing a twelve-starred crown – suggestive of her rule over the year. Her throne is surrounded by crops. The bolster on which she sits has a heart-shaped profile – an allusion to love and, by extension, fertility. A waterfall hints at the flow of life.

III – The **Empress**

Starting-points

- Appreciation of nature
- The relationship between the spiritual and physical worlds
- Nature's contradictions
- Transformation and creativity
- Appreciation of the feelings of others
- Maternal love may be both kind and possessive

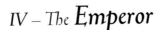

IV – The *Emperor*

The Emperor, symbol of earthly authority, is the most powerful representative of the outer world in the Major Arcana. He complements the Empress; his concerns are with authority and justice. The Emperor is stern and objective, and when meeting him as a traveller we must examine our own worldly life. Are we attentive toward the physical needs of others? – a question that complements the Empress' enquiry about our sensitivity to emotional needs. Are we contributing more to the physical world than we are taking away? Are we making the best use of the passing years?

As well as standing for earthly power, the Emperor represents courage and determination. Just as the Magician implied that the traveller must use the power of the will in the inner world, so the Emperor emphasizes the importance of the will in the outer world. He is the ideal of the wise and strong earthly leader, but like the Empress he can be cruel as well as kind. Masculine power can come to dominate, to be excessively authoritarian. The Emperor shows us the need for self-knowledge, for an awareness of the real motives behind our actions: he makes it clear that we must beware of misusing power and becoming selfish and egotistical.

Those in authority can be lonely unless they retain the ability to value and relate to those who serve them. Thus, the Emperor is shown in profile, half turning away from his subjects.

IV – The **Emperor**

Keywords

Authority

Justice

Thoughtfulness

Determination

Courage

Control

Self-knowledge

The Emperor: in detail

Orb and cross: Like the Empress, the Emperor carries the cross and orb on his staff, symbols of the heavenly and earthly worlds respectively – reminding us that humankind lives simultaneously in both worlds and must be in touch with them both to become whole.

Crown: The Emperor's crown rests on top of a soft hat, emphasizing the need to temper justice with mercy and also reminding us that authority rests on less firm foundations than we may suppose.

Shield: The Emperor's shield carries the same eagle as that of the Empress, but this eagle faces toward him rather than looking away – suggesting that his power resides in his own strength rather than, as with the Empress, in nature.

Castle: The Emperor's castle is set within the beauty of nature, suggesting a harmony between our own strength and the bounty of the natural world. But do the stones on the ground remind us, perhaps, that the castle's security comes from being unyielding?

Variations

• The Emperor's card shows few significant variations between different decks. Some decks, such as the Golden Dawn and the Rider-Waite, depict him full-face, but in most he is in profile.

IV – The Emperor

• The Tarot de Marseille portrays the Emperor with crown, orb and sceptre, and eagle shield, seated on a throne – this image is similar to the one shown here, the main difference being that Marseille has no landscape and no castle.

• The Rider-Waite Emperor is markedly severe: there is no lush greenery in this version, only stony determination. The rams' heads on his throne suggest thrusting potency, perhaps with connotations of magic; they may also allude to the zodiac (Aries, associated with the element fire and with Mars). He has no shield, but his legs are encased in armour – the suppression of the natural.

Starting-points

• Self-examination
• The finite nature of earthly life
• The need for a firm will, combined with flexibility
• The need for courage
• Masculine power may tend toward the despotic
• The loneliness of the ruler's role

V – The *Hierophant*

The Hierophant stands in much the same relation to the Emperor as the High Priestess stands to the Empress. Whereas the Emperor is masculine worldly power, the Hierophant is masculine spiritual power. This complements the feminine power of the High Priestess. The Hierophant completes a set of four cards that together represent the archetypal quadrant of spiritual and earthly power in both female and male aspects. This quadrant is one of the foundations of the Major Arcana, and sets much of the context for the whole deck.

The Hierophant is named in some decks as the High Priest, but this obscures the point that a Hierophant is a spiritual teacher as well as a priest. The High Priestess is the channel of spiritual wisdom; the Hierophant is the channel that interprets this wisdom and makes it understandable to us all. Here he is shown teaching, and if we become his pupils we are prompted to ask how much spiritual knowledge we possess and how much we use in our lives.

Like the High Priestess, the Hierophant is a rather remote figure. Much of what he says is not open to debate but comes with spiritual authority. He does not force anything upon listeners, or compel their obedience. They are free to accept or reject his teachings. But he does not compromise on what he knows to be the truth, nor does he pretend that the path he is describing is always easy.

Keywords

High Priest

Teacher

The Masculine

Knowledge

Authority

Interpretation

Truth

V – The *Hierophant*

The Hierophant: in detail

Hand: The palm of the Hierophant's right hand is held facing his heart, signifying that he must also keep some things hidden. He can show the way, but he will not reveal the destination. Some truths must be discovered rather than just described. The Maltese cross on the back of his hand is both a cross and a circle – symbolizing heaven and eternity.

Crown: The Hierophant's three-tiered crown represents sovereignty over the physical, mental and spiritual worlds. Similar symbolism is found in the triple cross that he holds in his left hand: this suggests the Holy Trinity, the three-fold nature of the spiritual realm.

Pillars: The two pillars behind the Hierophant hint at the majesty of the spiritual world. They could also be taken to refer to law and liberty or to sacrifice and purity – qualities required by all those who search for the truth.

Listeners: The Hierophant's listeners are three in number, reminiscent of the three Magi who travelled to Bethlehem for the birth of Jesus, drawn there by a star. They symbolize all seekers of true wisdom.

Variations

- The Hierophant is always shown as a spiritual or magical figure, but some decks ignore his function as a teacher.

- The Tarot de Marseille depicts a Pope (Pape), with two worshippers. One variant of this deck instead shows Jove (Jupiter) and his eagle.

- The Golden Dawn deck portrays the Hierophant holding a shepherd's crook, which introduces episcopal symbolism linking him with Christ as the Good Shepherd.

- The Aleister Crowley Thoth deck presents the Hierophant as a wizard, along with the four creatures of the Apocalypse (man, lion, bull and eagle) in the corners – in most decks these symbols appear only in Card XXI, The World.

- In the Rider-Waite deck the Hierophant has two priestly listeners, both male, and between them lie the keys of heaven at his feet.

V – The **Hierophant**

Starting-points

- The need for interpretation and understanding
- A genuine spiritual teacher speaks with authority
- How much spiritual knowledge do we have?
- We cannot compromise on the truth
- Some things must be discovered, not described
- Sacrifice is needed in the spiritual search

73

VI – The *Lovers*

After meeting the Magician and learning of the illusory nature of the physical world, and then meeting the female and male archetypes of spiritual and temporal power represented by the High Priestess and the Hierophant, the Empress and the Emperor, the Fool needs reassurance that their teachings have been understood. In symbolizing the potential union of female and male, the Lovers demonstrate that although many crucial decisions lie ahead, significant progress has been made.

Like all Major Arcana cards, the Lovers present a challenge as well as a lesson. They form an emotional triangle, with the feminine portrayed as both a chaste maiden (the spiritual path of the High Priestess) and a sensuous seductress (the worldly path of the Empress). Which should the young man choose? Or can all three unite in spiritual and physical harmony? Are the women distinct from each other, or are they aspects of the same reality? Above the man's head Cupid, symbolizing the emotions, draws his bow, but his blindfold shows that the dilemma cannot be solved by feelings alone.

The Lovers are therefore about the power of love, but also about the reconciliation of opposites, both within our psychological lives and in the outside world. Can seemingly opposing aspects of our nature and of our circumstances be reconciled and integrated into a harmonious whole to provide us with a more balanced way of dealing with life-experiences?

Keywords

Potential

Union

Challenge

Chaste / Sensuous

Choice

Opposites

Harmony

VI – The *Lovers*

The Lovers: in detail

Young man: The young man, loving both women, finds it hard to choose between them. He is fully clothed. Is he a stranger to himself? This is the first time since the Fool that the seeker himself appears in an image – unless we count the listeners in the Hierophant. The elaborate cravat may hint at the danger of vanity.

Cupid: Cupid's arrow is pointing at the youth himself – could this refer to the danger of self-love? The blindfold indicates emotions whose workings we cannot understand. The cloud obscuring the sun suggests mental confusion.

Seductress: The sensuous maiden may help the youth by releasing his emotional side and by teaching him the ways of the world. Being naked, she is vulnerable and exposed, and keeps nothing from him.

Virgin: The chaste maiden will give the youth help as he travels on the spiritual path. She is dressed and modest, yet at the same time she is the more secretive of the two women, hiding part of herself from the public gaze – and perhaps from his view also.

Variations

• The Tarot de Marseille shows the youth with two clothed women who are seeking his attention – they are not distinguished by any obvious symbolism, but a choice between virtue and vice may be intended. Cupid aims his arrow with the sun blazing behind him – light can be as confusing as mist.

VI – The *Lovers*

• Rider-Waite, in representing the lovers as Adam and Eve, reverts to the old Italian tradition of depicting a couple in this card rather than three figures. Above them an archangel, floating on a cloud, extends his hands in blessing, with the sun behind. Eve has the Tree of Knowledge behind her, with the serpent; Adam, the Tree of Life.

Starting-points

• The harmony that can come from a good decision
• The involvement of intellect and emotion in the choices we make
• Apparent opposites are sometimes two versions of the same thing
• We must avoid concealing ourselves from ourselves
• The complementary nature of inner and outer worlds

• The Golden Dawn Tarot shows a more extreme challenge, with a naked woman (Andromeda) chained to a rock and menaced by a dragon, while a figure with sword and shield (Perseus) descends from a cloud to rescue her.

VII – The Chariot

Of all the Major Arcana cards, the Chariot is most expressive of movement and speed, conveying the message that the traveller has passed through the preliminary stages of the journey and is now equipped to explore the deep mysteries ahead. The Chariot was the mythical vehicle of Ra, the Egyptian Sun God, and its presence in the Major Arcana not only symbolizes that the Fool is ready to proceed with his quest, but that he has already lost much of his foolishness. The process of transformation has begun.

The Chariot is also an archetype of the ascent of the spirit to heaven, assuring mortals that the spiritual path leads to eternal life. In Christianity the chariot also represents the Church. The Italian poet Dante Alighieri (1265–1321), in his allegorical portrayal of the journey through hell and purgatory to heaven (*The Divine Comedy*), refers to one wheel of the chariot as desire and will, and to the other as charity and prudence. Desire and will provide the motivation and strength to reach heaven, while charity and prudence represent universal love and compassionate concern. These are four qualities necessary to carry us to heaven.

The Chariot also reassures the traveller of the prospect of being carried when in difficulties. Meditating on the symbol helps him to reflect on his possession of the above four qualities and their development, and to renew the vision of a richer, more exalted dimension of existence.

VII – The **Chariot**

Keywords

Sun God

Ascent

Motivation

Strength

Love

Compassion

The Chariot: in detail

Crown: The charioteer's gold crown symbolizes masculinity, the sun and knowledge, while the waxing and waning moons that appear as epaulettes on his shoulders denote femininity and mystery.

Reins: The charioteer needs to use the reins skilfully to ensure that his steeds operate in perfect harmony with each other. This skill needs to be applied lightly and with subtlety: a slight movement of one of the hands in the wrong direction could make him veer off track.

Horses: One horse is white, the other black. They are pulling in different directions (a mistake in an early deck that has been copied in many later decks): this emphasizes the tension between their opposing qualities (heaven and earth, spirit and body, inner and outer, female and male) and the skill required to control them.

City: The walled city that the charioteer is leaving behind represents the splendours and temptations of the material world, which are now losing their hold. Perhaps there is a suggestion, too, of breaking away from the security of habit.

Variations

• The Visconti-Sforza version of this card shows a noblewoman in the chariot rather than a man – a processionary passenger rather than an active rider. The horses are winged. By the 18th century a male rider had become far more frequent.

• In the Tarot de Marseille the Chariot is moving at a stately pace, and the horses are both white. The crown and the lunar epaulettes are present, but there is no city.

• Rider-Waite has a pair of stately, static sphinxes, one black and one white, in place of the horses. The charioteer is crowned with a sunburst embellishment and the city is visible behind him.

• Aleister Crowley's Thoth deck shows four small, winged, mythical creatures, not in motion – perhaps suggesting, enigmatically, that the traveller's journey has come to a halt.

VII – *The* **Chariot**

Starting-points

• The transformation from ignorance to wisdom
• The reconciliation of opposites
• Existence has a rich and exalted dimension that we can glimpse
• The qualities we need to summon up that will enable us to ascend
• Looking back to see the distance travelled

VIII – *Strength*

Strength can have many meanings, but in most decks the symbolism is clear. A young woman is either subduing a lion or has a lion as a companion. The message is that true strength is the ability to grow in self-knowledge and become mistress or master of oneself.

Strength also carries a warning that the empowering nature of the earlier experiences of working with the Tarot should not be allowed to lead to feelings of spiritual pride. There is a risk that the progress made may feed the ego and lead to self-congratulation. The strongest adversary with whom we have to struggle in life is ourself.

Thus, the card shows the higher self, symbolized by the young woman, overcoming the lower emotional self, in the form of the lion. The lion is not evil and is a source of valuable, necessary energy. However, it must be tamed and used in the service of the higher self in order for the traveller to grow both psychologically and spiritually.

As well as the emotions, the lion symbolizes the other aspect of the self that frequently feeds the ego – the intellect. The mind can be tricked by its own powers into believing that intellect alone holds the key to life's mysteries. There are other ways of knowing, as we should have learned by now – for example, from the intuitive skills of the High Priestess. Strength shows that the intellect, like the emotions, should be used as the servant of the self and not as its master.

VIII – *Strength*

Keywords

Mastery

Submission

Spiritual pride

Emotions / Intellect

Ego

Empowerment

Gentleness

Strength: in detail

Hat: The brim of the young woman's hat is in the shape of the figure of eight, the symbol of infinity (which also appears on the Magician's hat), emphasizing her association with spiritual wisdom. Her arms encircle the lion, but gently and lovingly: strength does not come through brute force.

Lion's jaws: Is she holding the lion's mouth open or is she about to clamp it closed? The image is ambivalent – perhaps suggesting that she is encouraging the lion to give voice to certain feelings and to remain silent on others. The emotional self must exercise restraint when expressing itself.

Submissive posture: The lion submits willingly – the gentler side of emotion. The emotions are not merely primitive and amoral, as is sometimes thought. They include love, compassion and empathy, and are an essential part of what makes us human.

Rock: The rock in this card is bluish in hue and could just possibly be read as a stream or a lake. Perhaps this reminds us that water, though fluid, can be immensely strong – even stronger than rock.

Variations

• Early Italian decks present Fortezza (Fortitude) as a woman alongside a stone pillar, sometimes breaking it. A lion also appears in the card in a deck from Ferrara, dating from *c.*1470. Fortitude is one of the cardinal virtues, together with Temperance and Justice.

VIII – *Strength*

• The Visconti-Sforza version shows a man wielding a club to subdue a lion – such aggression is unusual in the Tarot.

• It was the Rider-Waite deck that made Strength card VIII – in previous decks Justice had occupied this position and Strength was XI. The woman who tames the lion has an infinity symbol above her head, and she holds a wreath of flowers, which are a commonly found feature in this card.

• Aleister Crowley's Thoth Tarot calls this card Lust in its modern version. The woman who dares to approach the lion is naked.

Starting-points

• The lightest of touches can be a source of true strength
• The risks of self-congratulation when progress is made
• The strongest adversary is ourself
• The gentler side of the emotions
• The intellect is not the only way of knowing

IX – The *Hermit*

The Hermit is a transitional card, indicating that the traveller is about to enter a more enigmatic, demanding phase of the journey. The card symbolizes the truth that many insights can only be discovered through quiet contemplation, away from human society.

Significantly, nine, the number of this card, is the product of 3 x 3 (three being the basis of the Trinity, and the prime spiritual number), with connotations of eternal life. The card therefore has life-enhancing powers.

The Hermit shines light in dark places because he carries the message that solitude, silence and meditation are essential aids to spiritual progress. Solitude takes us away from the multiple distractions of the material world; silence enables us to become aware of ourself and our own reality; while meditation allows us to turn the mind inward and become receptive to the subtle wisdom that arises from the collective unconscious and from the mysterious reaches beyond even this.

We all have the Hermit within us. There is an element of isolation even in our intimate relationships: although we may bond with another, we can never fuse with another. Yet many of us grow up without any real sense of what it means to enjoy our own company. Thus, the symbol of the Hermit, with its attendant lessons, is particularly appropriate for us, living as we do amid the sensory overload of our modern existence.

IX – The **Hermit**

Keywords

Solitude

Silence

Meditation

Self-denial

Awareness

Self-containment

The Hermit: in detail

Lamp: The Hermit carries a lamp, both to illuminate his own path and as a guiding light to those who might wish to follow in his footsteps. Light, in its double aspect of search and revelation, is a constant theme in spiritual and mystical literature. The star hints at spiritual significance; the moon suggests illumination of a heavenly nature.

Staff: This is another symbol frequently associated with the search for revelation and spiritual truth. Pilgrims carry staffs on their long journeys to holy places, and the staff serves as a means of both support and protection. It also symbolizes the association between humankind and nature. In addition, it represents trust and companionship.

Hood and cape: The Hermit's monkish robe and hood suggest austerity, while the hood also signifies secrecy and the rejection of vanity.

Sandals: A pair of sandals is characteristic of the garb of both hermits and pilgrims, representing material poverty and a willingness to suffer if necessary on the stony path to enlightenment.

Variations

- Most Tarot decks, influenced by the Tarot de Marseille, show the Hermit as an old man, often bearded and stooping – emphasizing that he is the archetype of the Wise Old Man, in Jungian terms. The lamp, staff, robe and sandals feature in most decks, and the Hermit is typically on a journey rather than secluded in a cave.

IX – The *Hermit*

- A few early Italian versions, including the Visconti-Sforza, show the Hermit with an hourglass instead of a lantern.

- The Rider-Waite Hermit looks especially lonely – he stands on what may be a mountain peak (there are mountains in the distance too), surrounded by nothing but sky.

- The pillar behind the man in some decks warns us not to imagine that he is powerless: the apparent physical fragility may disguise a great source of energy.

Starting-points

- The conditions for finding inner wisdom
- Stripping the self down to its essentials in search of profound truths
- Antidotes to vanity
- The wise old man and what he can teach us
- The discoveries that a pilgrim can make on an inward journey

89

X – *The* **Wheel** *of* **Fortune**

The wheel, like the circle, is a sacred symbol in many cultures, but whereas the circle is a static image, without beginning or end and suggestive of infinity and eternity, the wheel is dynamic and represents change and movement, the cycle of birth and death.

When represented as the Wheel of Fortune, the wheel symbolizes the changing circumstances that attend each individual life – sometimes good, sometimes bad. It also poses the question: why should things be this way? We are reminded that progress on the path does not mean that we are able to step off the Wheel of Fortune. Seemingly bad things happen to good people and seemingly good things happen to bad people. What is the purpose of all this? Who or what is responsible? Who turns the handle on the wheel?

The Wheel of Fortune leaves us to ponder these questions. Are we to blame for our good and bad fortune? Perhaps God or some other supernatural force determines our luck on the basis of our behaviour, as punishment or reward? Or perhaps we are judged by the degree of courage or stoicism we show when Fortune turns against us? For the enlightened mind, everything that happens to us offers lessons to be learned, and it could be that our present powers of understanding are inadequate to grasp the underlying purpose behind events – the "will of God". This world of changing fortunes is where people are put to the test and may grow.

Keywords

Mutability

Vicissitudes

Cycle

Destiny

Experience

Challenge

X – The *Wheel* of *Fortune*

The Wheel of Fortune: in detail

Wheel: This is one of the most transforming of all human inventions, carrying us among the hazards of life, and symbolizing movement and change. Can we ourselves turn the handle?

Sphinx: At the top of the wheel is a sphinx, representing wisdom. Our desire for wisdom may take us to a position of apparent supremacy, but can we stay there?

Monkey: Wilfulness may overcome wisdom, identifying us with the monkey – wayward, unpredictable and capable of mischief, not always intended as such.

Hare: Leaping about in an erratic fashion, the hare represents our changeable nature. In some cultures the hare signifies lustful vitality.

Pyramids: In this design the wheel is supported on pyramids, or triangles, decorated with stars, and is independent of planet Earth. Perhaps the ultimate destination is the heavens, to which the triangles point? The stars within the triangles might support this interpretation.

Variations

• There are many variations between decks in the Wheel of Fortune, and it is not always easy to see the purpose of the symbolism.

• Blindfolded Fortune, represented as a lady, turns the Wheel in some representations, including some of the early Italian decks.

• The Tarot de Marseille is the inspiration for the card shown here, with sphinx, monkey and hare, and a handle on the wheel.

X – The **Wheel** of **Fortune**

• The Rider-Waite deck shows not a wheel but a circle decorated with hermetic symbols and surrounded in space by the symbols of the four Evangelists (lion, ox, man, eagle), all winged. On the right of the "wheel" is the Egyptian jackal-headed deity Anubis; to the left is a tumbling snake, representing Typhon, father of all monsters in Greek myth; on top is an Egyptian Sphinx. ROTA, inscribed on the wheel, is almost an anagram of Tarot.

Starting-points

• Fortune spreads its blessings and its trials without regard for moral distinctions
• The challenge of being at the mercy of chance
• How our state of mind can transform the experience of good and bad luck
• Development may depend upon our ability to cope with change

XI – *Justice*

In the Sephiroth, the Kabbalistic Tree of Life (see pages 42–5), Justice is paired with Mercy, the point being that these two qualities should be held in balance. In terms of the balance of male and female, it may be inferred that Justice is male and Mercy female, but in fact Justice is traditionally the woman. She is often depicted holding scales, and sometimes blindfolded to show impartiality.

In Greek mythology Themis is the goddess of justice, often shown holding a sword to symbolize the spiritual power dividing heaven and earth. The sword is also a symbol for justice in Judeo-Christianity: after banishing Adam and Eve for disobedience, God sent a flaming sword to guard the gateway to Eden to prevent their return. In the Major Arcana Justice signifies not only justice but the importance of good judgment. At this point we are asked to judge our own actions, motivation, honesty and integrity. Spiritually advanced individuals are expected to live up to high standards of behaviour. Furthermore, they are expected to show perceptive judgment of others. In Zen Buddhism the Zen Master is said to recognize even without words the degree of enlightenment reached by pupils.

Justice is not, however, about the threat of rejection and punishment for those found wanting. It is a reminder of the importance of self-appraisal. In any assessment of self or others, justice and mercy are two sides of the same coin.

Keywords

Impartiality

Mercy

Decisiveness

Judgment

Integrity

Perception

Self-appraisal

XI – *Justice*

Justice: in detail

 Shell: The shell, which appears as a canopy above Justice's throne, is a traditional Western symbol of pilgrimage, and hence of endurance and effort.

 Red robe: Justice wears the red robe of earthly power, and perhaps also sacrifice (blood) – in contrast to the blue of the room, which represents spirituality.

 Scales: Justice holds the scales, symbolizing sound and impartial judgment. They are an attribute of Themis, Greek goddess of law and order.

 Sword: The sword stands not only for decisive justice, cleanly administered, but also for the ability to cut through ignorance and deceit.

 Throne: The pillars at either side of the throne of Justice are symbolic of the necessary balance between justice and mercy. Without this balance, harmony and peace in this world are impossible to find. The pillars also imply imposing authority derived from tradition: where precisely, we should ask ourselves, does the power of justice come from?

Variations

• The Visconti-Sforza Justice, from an early Italian deck, has a knight on horseback above the figure of Justice herself seated on her throne.

• In the Tarot de Marseille (as in earlier decks), Justice is similar in design to the card shown here, except that the scales and sword are in opposite hands, and the throne has no shell canopy or pillars.

XI – *Justice*

Starting-points

• The need for balance between justice and mercy
• The importance of carefully assessing our own motives and behaviour
• How can the spiritual divide between heaven and earth be crossed?
• Judgment starts with the self
• Essential standards of behaviour

• Rider-Waite's Justice follows Marseille, but the figure is a touch androgynous – though more male than female. The two pillars of the throne are clearly depicted. There is no shell canopy. Rider-Waite was the first deck to give Justice the number XI, reversing its position with Strength, which now became VIII.

• In Aleister Crowley's Thoth Tarot the card for Justice or Adjustment features the sword and scales imposed on top of each other, in an abstract arrangement.

XII – The *Hanged Man*

The Hanged Man, Card XII, is followed by Death, Card XIII. Together these cards mark a major transition in the Tarot journey. The traveller has now passed the mid-point in the Major Arcana and these cards test the progress made. Even in the earliest decks the Hanged Man is shown upside down, a punishment accorded to debtors in medieval Europe. What debt has the Hanged Man incurred? And why, in spite of his uncomfortable position, is his face serene?

The debt is incurred when we accept the gift of life. Life is given to us with conditions attached. We are expected to repay the debt by leaving the world a better place than we find it. This can be expressed in terms of an obligation to the divine: "Life is your gift from God; what you make of it is your gift *to* God." Even though the Hanged Man has not yet repaid his debt, his calm expression shows that he is doing so. The trees symbolize the Tree of Knowledge and the Tree of Life, and both are showing the green shoots of spring. The Hanged Man's hair floats halo-like around his head, and if he were upright his crossed legs would show the sign of four, the sign of completion. He is not yet upright and completion is yet to come; but the potential for it is clear.

The Hanged Man's reversed position has a further symbolic meaning. His old world-view, which saw materialism as superior to spirituality, has now been turned upside down.

Keywords

Obligation

Upside down

Completion

Serene

Heaven / Earth

Transfiguration

Springtime

XII – The **Hanged Man**

The Hanged Man: in detail

Two trees: The Tree of Knowledge and the Tree of Life feature in the Garden of Eden. Eve's disobedience in eating the forbidden fruit of the former, and God's resolve to prevent them from eating the fruit of the latter, were the reasons for their ejection from the Garden. But the green shoots hint that these restrictions on knowledge and life may apply only in the material world. The spiritual world promises more: supreme wisdom and eternal life.

Nimbus: The Hanged Man is suspended between heaven and earth, symbolizing our dual existence between two worlds – although in our ignorance we tend to pay attention only to the earth. We cannot see the heavens clearly if we are hanging upside down. However, the nimbus suggests that this man has potential for transfiguration – on account of martyrdom?

One leg: The incomplete wisdom of the Hanged Man is emphasized by the fact that he hangs from only one leg, representing his attachment to material existence. His other leg, which remains free, symbolizes his spiritual self, unfettered to the physical world. The man looks to be in profound discomfort, but could that impression be false?

Variations

- The card shown here adopts the features of the Tarot de Marseille, including the two trees, the arrangement of the legs, and the hands behind the back – but in the early French card what *could* be interpreted as a burst of light around the head could also, more mundanely, be falling yellow hair; and the trees have little stumps rather than sprouting foliage.

- Some modern decks (such as the Rider-Waite) reverse the order in which the legs are crossed, so that the number four is more explicitly suggested. This is a pity, as it removes the suggestion of incompleteness.

- In the Thoth Tarot the Hanged Man is naked, a symbol of vulnerability: he has discarded the old and is ready to put on the new.

- A few recent decks show radical variations. For example, one depicts a stage magician immersed head down in a tank of water.

XII – The **Hanged Man**

Starting-points

- The uses we are making of the gift of life itself
- We live between two worlds – at which of them are we looking?
- Our movement toward completion
- The concepts that are turned upside down by spiritual progress
- Knowledge and life at their most vigorous

XIII – Death

Death is an inescapable fact of life, but all major spiritual traditions teach that far from being the end, death is a transition to new and grander possibilities. But at the same time all traditions teach that the progress, or lack of it, that we make in this life is important in determining the nature of our posthumous experiences.

Looked at in this way, Card XIII, Death, gives us important opportunities to reassess our attitudes to life and death. There is nothing alarming about the card, which is about change and transition. Its message is positive and optimistic, and further emphasizes the lessons of the Hanged Man while adding a further lesson – that of rebirth. We should not wait for actual death in order to be reborn. In a sense we are "reborn" each morning when we greet the new day, and each rebirth provides us with a fresh start as well as symbolizing the major rebirths that await us when we fully recognize that we are spiritual beings, and when we finally leave the physical world at the end of our time here.

Death also stands for the opportunity to discard much of the mental and emotional baggage that we carry with us in life. It is this baggage, composed of traumatic or unhappy memories, resentments, frustrations, and so on, that is responsible for many psychological problems. All psychotherapies, and many religions, teach the importance of putting down this self-imposed burden.

XIII – *Death*

Keywords

Transition

Letting go

Loss / Gain

Reassessment

Optimism

Rebirth

Catharsis

Death: in detail

 Skeleton: Death is traditionally shown as an archetypal skeleton, symbolizing the loss of material goods and the fact that even without these goods life goes on.

 Hood: Death is a hooded figure, a traditional symbol conveying the message that mortality is inscrutable: we do not know how and when death will make its appearance, but there could well be an element of disguised harm.

 Scythe: The skeleton carries a scythe, because death cuts our emotional ties with the physical world. We should consider what remains of us when these ties are gone. Could there be an element of liberation in the process?

 Heads: These remnants of the physical body conjure up humanity at its most basic: kings and queens meet with the same death as their subjects.

 River: This feature is Lethe, famed river of forgetfulness in the life to come, but is it also perhaps a subtle reminder that the flow of life continues endlessly in the place that we have left behind?

Variations

• In most versions of the Tarot de Marseille the name, Death, is missing from the XIIIth card, probably for superstitious reasons. The reaper with his scythe looks monstrously grim but is not straightforwardly skeletal. He has just lopped off two hands, which spout blood.

• Many early Italian versions show the reaping skeleton on a pale horse on a terrain strewn with body parts (including those of slain Arcana). Alternatively, Death is shown as an archer.

• Rider-Waite shows an armoured skeleton on horseback, suggestive of the Four Horsemen of the Apocalypse (Famine, Plague, War and Death). He rides across a battlefield where the king lies slain and he carries a black banner on which a mystic rose is depicted – symbol of rebirth. There are three living people in the card: a distraught maiden, a curious child and a bishop. The latter figure is suggestive of unwavering faith.

XIII – Death

Starting-points

• Ending as beginning
• The benefits of an inner purge or cull
• Rebirth in this life comes with the realization that we are spiritual beings
• The shedding of useless psychological baggage
• Universal experiences, from birth to death
• Life's endless flow

XIV – *Temperance*

Temperance means moderation, the ability to take a careful course between two extremes. The Temple of Apollo at Delphi, one of the most famous shrines in the ancient world, carried the inscription "Moderation in all things", while the Buddhist doctrine of the Middle Way teaches a similarly thoughtful approach: maintain a balance between opposing energies, do not surrender your powers of discrimination and do not lose your sense of proportion.

In the Major Arcana, Temperance cautions the traveller not to get carried away by progress made so far. A balance must be kept between what has been done and what remains to be done. We must not be deluded by our achievements, or believe that we have a monopoly on the truth. On the spiritual path there is a danger of acquiring an inflated sense of superiority. Above all, we must avoid fanaticism. The wise man listens to and respects the views of others, and does not rush to argue or belittle.

Temperance, like Justice, reminds us of the importance of keeping an equilibrium, between the conscious and the unconscious minds, between the outer and inner worlds, between head and heart, soul and body, male and female aspects of being. When we allow ourselves, spiritually, mentally or physically, to become stuck in an entrenched position, the Buddha-mind (the enlightened mind that appraises reality objectively) is lost.

Keywords

Moderation

Route-finding

Equilibrium

Proportion

Peace

Virtue

Water / Wine

XIV – Temperance

Temperance: in detail

Angelic figure: A winged figure with a nimbus pours water from one pitcher into another. The angelic connotations are appropriate, as temperance is associated with peace and fairness. Conflict arises when temperance is abandoned.

Stream of water: Pouring water from one pitcher to another represents the maintenance of equilibrium. Neither pitcher is allowed to become full at the expense of the other. The person creating the balance has to be active (compare scales), even though some may think of temperance as a passive virtue. The water is common to both pitchers: there may be more similarity between opposing forces than we realize.

Two pitchers: The upper pitcher (gold in this design) symbolizes the spiritual and the lower pitcher (iron) the material world. Both share in the same essence of being, like the soul and the body, the head and the heart.

Corn: If water is conserved (a full pitcher may overflow), the result will be a spiritual harvest. All that is needed to ensure this outcome is to be found in nature – symbolized by the irrigating stream.

Variations

- Most decks show this card as a woman pouring water from one receptacle to another: the time-honoured image of Temperance as one of the cardinal virtues. Originally, this symbol was intended to refer to the dilution of wine by the addition of water.

- In the Tarot de Marseille and other early decks, Temperance is the only one of the cardinal virtues consistently to have wings.

XIV – *Temperance*

- In Rider-Waite, as in many other decks, the figure has one foot in the water, as if to indicate that she is at home in both material and spiritual worlds. As with the image shown here, the sun in Rider-Waite is prominent in a cloudless sky, and is close to the horizon: is it rising or setting? It conceals a crown – a reference to the victory over the ego.

- In Aleister Crowley's Thoth Tarot, this card is called Art rather than Temperance.

Starting-points

- The dangers of extremes and imbalances
- Temperance and commitment – can dilution be a virtue?
- Does the truth always lie between opposing views?
- The complementarity of the spiritual and material

XV – The *Devil*

The devil was regarded for centuries as an objective force for evil, usually personified as a horned, cloven-footed being, reminiscent of Pan, the ancient Greek god of the amoral forces of nature. In some forms of Christian belief, however, the devil was seen as Lucifer, a fallen angel who was expelled from heaven for challenging God's authority, although this view arises from a mistaken interpretation of Isaiah 14:12, "How art thou fallen from Heaven, O Lucifer, son of the morning!"

In the Tarot the devil is seen more in terms of Kabbalistic and other schools of Jewish thought, which regard him as a sort of quality control, a force that tests us to see what we are made of.

Without such a negative force there would be nothing to strive against, and therefore nothing to help us to progress spiritually. In this sense, the request in the Lord's Prayer that God "lead us not into temptation" is a plea not to put us to tests beyond our strength.

In Jungian psychology the devil is sometimes identified with the shadow side of human nature – this is the side that prompts us into negative behaviour, that we often try to hide away, even from ourselves, instead of facing and transforming into a positive force – much as we can transform anger into determination. With this in mind, the Tarot Devil should be seen as a power to be confronted and overcome, a test to be passed – rather than as an evil to be feared.

Keywords

Pan

Fallen angel

Trial of strength

Tests / Temptations

Progress

Shadow

Transformation

XV – The *Devil*

The Devil: in detail

Horned head: The ram's horns recall Pan, the Greek nature god. Yet nature can be commandeered for dubious purposes. Brute appetites are dangerous: what, we should ask ourselves, have we learned from Temperance?

Pentangle: The upside-down pentangle denotes evil: the devil's horns pointing perversely and blasphemously to heaven. We must check our motives for following the spiritual path: could it be that the ego is at work?

Torch: Apparently illuminating, the torch is also a tool of destruction. It suggests an invitation to visit the darkest places of the self – can we resist this temptation?

Hand: The Devil holds up one of his hands, as if to halt progress. This left hand warns the traveller not to follow the left-hand path, the path of evil and of "black" magic.

Chained figures: The two chained naked figures have failed the Devil's tests and have thus become enslaved to him. The horns on their heads show the corruption of the self when the wrong path is chosen.

Variations

- In the Tarot de Marseille the Devil is shown as an androgynous figure, with male genitals and female breasts. Some of the body parts are seen in the wrong places: for example, a mouth on the stomach and an extra pair of eyes in the knees. He has the bat-like wings that appear in most later versions.

XV – The *Devil*

- The Rider-Waite Devil is similar to the image shown here, except that the devil holds a downward-pointing torch in his left hand. The chained figures are more devil-like, with tails as well as horns. The model for this basic design (although without the torch and without the two victims) is a mid-19th-century illustration by the French magician Eliphas Levi, showing a pagan idol known as the Baphomet.

- In Aleister Crowley's Thoth Tarot, the subject is a ram with massive twisted double horns. Below, in golden bubbles, are human figures writhing in hellish torment.

Starting-points

- The idea of the devil as a test of our goodness
- Negative forces give us something to strive against
- Identifying our shadow side
- Our motives for following a spiritual path should be examined
- The dangers of succumbing to temptation

XVI – The *Tower*

At first sight the Tower appears particularly enigmatic. A man and a woman are falling from a tower that appears to have been struck by lightning. What exactly is happening? Together with Death and the Devil, the Tower completes a trio of potentially rather threatening cards. However, as with Death and the Devil, the Tower's symbolism is not negative – although it is more open to personal interpretation than any other card in the Major Arcana.

For some the Tower is the dark night of the soul, the experience described by mystics in which the spiritual revelations are abruptly withdrawn, leaving a feeling of loss and desolation. This experience is not confined to mystics. Having felt uplifted psychologically and spiritually by the growth of spiritual awareness, the individual can, for no apparent reason, find him or herself entering a barren period, when awareness seems lost, usually temporarily. However, a more constructive interpretation is that the Tower represents the destruction of illusions, spiritual pride and beliefs in false gods.

The lightning striking the tower supports this interpretation. It destroys but also illuminates. The way ahead becomes clearer. And like the fire that can follow, lightning can purify and cleanse by consuming the old and decaying, and clearing the ground for fresh growth. The fall from the Tower and the loss of old certainties may be superficially painful, but the two figures will come to no harm.

Keywords

Disturbance

Falling

Illumination

Ego

Destruction / Creation

Release

Purification

XVI – The Tower

The Tower: in detail

Tower: This symbol is seen as phallic by some Tarot commentators – but the falling people are clothed, which makes that interpretation unlikely. The Tower may be the proud ego and its delusional certainties.

Lightning: The bolt of lightning that destroys the Tower may suggest divine justice. If we stray from our spiritual roots, whatever we build will not endure.

Sun: This suggests divine bounty, the bottomless well of cosmic creation. The sun's power is inexhaustible, which makes it a suitable analogy for the spirit or for love.

Golden rain: A regenerative energy can follow destruction. The image of golden raindrops falling from the sun has overtones of the miraculous.

Builders: The falling man and woman are the builders of the Tower. They had not yet fully relinquished the materialism of bricks and stones. But finally they abandon their mistaken ideas. Another interpretation might be that the figures are prisoners, who have been released by a natural disaster.

Variations

- Some early painted decks such as the Visconti-Sforza do not include this card.

- In at least one early printed deck a similar idea is conveyed by two naked lovers fleeing a burning building (recalling Adam and Eve being expelled from the Garden of Eden).

XVI – The Tower

- The Tarot de Marseille equivalent is La Maison de Dieu (House of God). The lightning has a feathery quality, as if unexpectedly benign. The Tower has three windows but no door – hinting at the difficulty of exiting the ego's fabrications once they are erected. The two figures tumble toward the earth – there is no sea and no river. A large crown has been dislodged from the summit of the edifice.

- Rider-Waite's Tower resembles the Marseille version but is in darkness – the "dark night of the soul". Flames emerge from each window. The falling figures are a king and a queen.

Starting-points

- The shattering of the ego's certainties
- The Tower of Babel – a monument to human pride and pretension
- That which destroys can also liberate and illuminate
- Expulsion from the earthly kingdom
- The growth that can follow destruction

XVII – The *Star*

Having completed the trilogy of Death, the Devil and the Tower, a celestial trilogy now welcomes the traveller. The first part of the trio is the Star, followed by the Moon and the Sun.

The Star is one of the most gracious of all the Tarot cards. It was supposedly a star that guided the Magi to the birthplace of Christ, and having come through the various stages of the Tarot, the traveller is now blessed with the guidance of the Star.

In the form of the five-pointed pentangle, the star is in many cultures an archetypal symbol for enlightenment; while the six-pointed star, the combination of upward-pointing male triangle and downward-pointing female triangle, is the symbol of creation, conception and birth. The star shines in the night sky, but its light is subtle and not as easily discerned as that of the sun and the moon. The traveller has to scan the heavens. Finding a star requires discrimination and commitment.

The star the traveller seeks is best represented by the Pole Star, the symbol of constancy and of eternity, a still pivotal point in the celestial panoply, and thus regarded by the ancients as the gate of heaven itself.

Now that the traveller has at last reached the Star, a particularly propitious moment has come. Stars tend to be awarded as a sign of achievement, and the traveller can reflect on this achievement before embarking on the final stages of the journey.

XVII – The *Star*

Keywords

Revelation

Guidance

Perfection

Serenity

Auspiciousness

Eternity

Attainment

The Star: in detail

Pitchers: The obvious comparison is with Temperance (see pages 106–109), another card showing a woman with two pitchers. Here, instead of pouring water from one pitcher to the other, she pours both into the river. The balance symbolized by Temperance has now been fully achieved. The water in the pitchers thus signifies the living streams of the collective unconscious and of spiritual wisdom.

Bird in tree: Near the woman, on the opposite bank of the river, is the Tree of Life, with a bird in its canopy (sometimes interpreted as an ibis) portraying the spiritual self, waiting to drink from the living waters.

Stars: The big star above the woman is surrounded by seven smaller ones, the number seven combining the three of the heavens and the four of the earth.

Naked woman: The woman's nakedness indicates the fact that many mysteries are now revealed to the traveller. Her beauty represents perfection and her smile is one of gentleness and peace. She is in tune with the mysteries, a person fulfilled, awakened and serene.

Variations

- Early cards showed simply a woman (or sometimes a man) looking at or pointing to a star. When a man on horseback is depicted beneath a bright star, this is probably a biblical reference to the Magi.

- The card illustrated is very close in its basic ingredients (naked woman, two pitchers pouring water, eight stars, bird in tree) to the Tarot de Marseille version.

XVII – The Star

- The Star in Rider-Waite is true to this design, except that the woman pours water from one pitcher onto the ground, symbolizing the conscious mind being fed by the living stream. A.E. Waite associated the main star with the Flaming Star found in Masonic temples. He said that the figure is "the Great Mother in the Kabbalistic Sephira Binah, which is supernal Understanding, who communicates to the Sephiroth that are below in the measure that they can receive her influx."

Starting-points

- Guidance from above, and the journey that ensues
- The pledge of eternity
- The star as a symbol of perfection and attainment
- Emptying the mind and self
- The suggestion that all will be well
- The subtle illumination of starlight

121

XVIII – The *Moon*

The moon is traditionally regarded as a feminine symbol. The ancient Egyptians and other early cultures observed that, unlike the sun, the moon changes both its shape and its position in the sky, and this fickle behaviour was thought to be a characteristic of the female sex. The association with femininity was further enhanced by the moon's association with the night, and therefore with mystery and hidden things.

The middle card in the celestial trio, the Moon indicates that the journey is nearing completion as the moon is waxing toward the full. The Moon also stands for psychic abilities, which are said to develop spontaneously as the individual progresses spiritually. But the card is not entirely positive. In the foreground a crayfish, symbol of the destructive aspect of the female, emerges from the waters of the unconscious, and two dogs – one the black dog that accompanied the Fool – bay at the moon. The crayfish reminds us that psychic abilities, which are traditionally associated with the female, can be diversions and even hindrances on the spiritual path, strengthening negative qualities such as pride and the appetite for power.

The pale dog guards the boundary between the physical and spiritual worlds and may also be destructive in that it can prevent the traveller from proceeding further. This is the point at which many seekers lose their way and fall into self-aggrandisement and delusion.

XVIII – The **Moon**

Keywords

Mystery

Inconstancy

Psychic powers

Ambiguity

Obstacles

Diversions

The Moon: in detail

Moon: The crescent moon sheds some light, yet there is still a sense of mystery. The clarity promised by the Star is still withheld: the moon is more secretive in her wisdom. Some things may forever remain beyond our limited understanding.

Towers: The two towers recall card XVI (The Tower), but now they represent the balance achieved in the Star and the resolution of opposites noted in the Lovers (card VI). The lofty top tier of the Tower destroyed by the lightning in card XVI has not been replaced: these new towers, no longer defensive bastions to preserve delusions, are landmarks that show the way forward.

Path: The path leads from the waters of the unconscious, fed by the living stream poured into them by the Star, toward the towers and the far horizon. The dogs may complicate the traveller's progress.

Crayfish: The crayfish lives in the watery realm of intuition, yet needs a shell to protect itself and pincers for attack. What destructive forces threaten it? What might be the object of its annihilating power? Does the creature work for good or evil?

Variations

• The old Italian decks depict a moon with an astrologer beneath it, doing lunar calculations; or else a woman holding up the moon.

• In later cards showing the two dogs, the paler dog is often interpreted, but rarely specifically recognizable, as a wolf.

• The card shown here shares its basic design with the Tarot de Marseille version, except that the French image shows no path. The path was probably added to link confusingly disparate items by the implied narrative of the quest.

• The towers in Rider-Waite are foreboding monolithic pillars, each with a tiny window at the top – some commentators interpret them as tombstones. The moon emanates golden drops of light, or "fertilizing dew", as Waite puts it: these also appear in the Marseille deck. Waite interprets this card as the imagination, as distinct from the life of the spirit.

XVIII – *The* **Moon**

Starting-points

• The illumination and concealment of moonlight
• Navigating among confusions
• The wisdom still hidden from the seeker
• A surreal landscape behind the veil of the mundane
• Can intuition be a dangerous power?

XIX – The Sun

Throughout much of recorded history the sun has been identified with the masculine principle, just as the moon is identified with the feminine. It follows a consistent course through the heavens and is forever present in the light of day. While the creativity of the moon takes place in darkness and secrecy, that of the sun takes place openly, in daylight. The moon is introverted, the sun extroverted.

In the Major Arcana this dual symbolism refers to the complementary nature of female and male, and by extension to the complementary relationship of introvert intuition and extrovert reason, of the unconscious and conscious minds, of inner and outer worlds, of the spiritual and the material. We can never be whole within ourselves unless these forces are in harmony and communication with each other. Without this wholeness a person will remain alienated and a stranger even to themselves.

The traveller is now on the point of realizing this wholeness. In place of dogs baying at the moon, the Sun portrays two lovers drawing together in union, their nakedness symbolic of openness, self-surrender, trust and commitment. Each body is given to the other. The journey is now nearing its fulfilment. There is one more trial ahead, but this will be one of surrender, not of effort. The work has been done, the effort has been made, and unconditional love is revealed as the source of all that is.

XIX – The *Sun*

Keywords

Extrovert / Introvert

Inexhaustible

Life-giving

Communication

Commitment

Trust

Self-surrender

The Sun: in detail

Sun: As supreme source of light, the sun is identified in many traditions with divinity, and mystics typically tell of visions of light. It is life's indispensable power-station, and infinite in its beneficence – reinforcing the circle as a symbol of infinity.

Lovers: The sun gives life and light impartially to the just and the unjust, and the lovers cannot simply be passive in their acceptance of its gifts. Free will requires that they put their blessings to good purpose, rather than misusing them. The woman's coronet of leaves is perhaps a good omen.

Sunflowers: The sunflower turns its flowerhead to follow the sun, and therefore has been seen as a symbol of reverence – a due recognition of the spirit. The form that this reverence takes is chosen by the lovers, in an exertion of free will.

Wall: The wall beyond the two lovers indicates the boundary separating heaven and earth. It is low enough to provide glimpses of the beyond, but high enough to be a significant barrier. The wall is also reminiscent of the expulsion of Adam and Eve from the Garden of Eden: perhaps the lovers here can avoid spiritual transgression?

Variations

- In the Visconti-Sforza deck the sun is held up by a naked figure who hovers above a dark cloud. The sun has a human face, as in later versions of this Major Arcana card.

- The Tarot de Marseille sets the basic design of later decks, with wall, anthropomorphic sun, and two lovers (with loin cloths). No flowers appear in this version. The sun sprays out droplets of light, in a style comparable to that of the Moon in the same deck.

XIX – The **Sun**

- The Sun of the Rider-Waite deck shows a single cherub on horseback, carrying a large red scrolling standard, perhaps symbolizing sacrifice – the blood of renewal. The sun with a human face, the wall and the sunflowers also feature in this card.

- The ethereal Aleister Crowley Thoth deck shows two winged cherubs gambolling playfully in the air.

Starting-points

- The wholeness that depends upon harmony between opposites
- Unconditional love as the source of all good things
- The energy that provides the food of life in an endless supply
- The sun giving its light impartially to all
- Glimpses beyond the wall

xx – Judgment

Having almost reached the destination and recently enjoyed the confirmation given by the celestial trilogy of Star, Moon and Sun, the traveller finds with a shock that the next card is Judgment. Why should we be judged at this late stage? What in any case does judgment involve?

The card would have come as no surprise to the medieval mind, which regarded judgment as an unavoidable part of life's journey. For us today the card is a necessary reminder that life is continual learning, and that at some point we must be tested on what has been learned. In the symbolism of the Tarot, such testing is not a prelude to eternal damnation or immediate heavenly bliss but a way of identifying in ourselves the lessons arising not only from the journey through the Major Arcana but from the cradle onward. We need to recognize the good we have done in the world and acknowledge and repent the harm. Hence, Judgment symbolizes the culmination of the quest for self-knowledge rather than the medieval fear of hell-fire.

Judgment is a time both for looking back at the distance travelled and for assessing the place at which we have arrived. The Tarot tells us that the more work there is done in this life, the easier it will be to handle the most testing questions we ever have to face. The truth is that our fate lies within ourselves, and that Judgment is more about our level of self-knowledge than about guilt or punishment.

Keywords

Evaluation

Stocktaking

Past / Future

Questions

Lessons

Self-knowledge

Wisdom

XX – *Judgment*

Judgment: in detail

Archangel: A winged archangel emerges from the clouds. This herald of Judgment is often identified with Gabriel – when we remember that Gabriel in the Christian story brings news of a great birth, fascinating parallels come to mind.

Trumpet: This is the archetypal wake-up call. Perhaps there are certain events in our life that have roused us from our moral or spiritual slumbers. Are there any such events that might await us in the future?

Graves: The grave is our last mortal resting place, but it might also be seen as a symbol of the unawakened state – the dormancy into which we might fall if we fail to pursue enlightenment. The claustrophobia of the grave might come from not reaching out to others, and to heaven.

Resurrection: The opening of graves and the resurrection of the dead prelude the summons before the Almighty on the Day of Judgment. The nakedness of the figures reflects the fact that nothing can be hidden from the divine eye. Most Christian thinkers accept that the resurrection refers to the spiritual, not the physical, body.

Variations

• The Visconti-Sforza Judgment shows two
  archangels, with God above them. Beneath,
  three naked awakened corpses are sitting in
  one grave, as if sharing a bath.

• Judgment in the Tarot de Marseille version
  shows three naked resurrected figures in the
  foreground of the image. A banner depicting
  the cross of St George hangs from the
  archangel's trumpet.

• The Rider-Waite version also includes the
  St George's cross banner. In the foreground
  are a resurrected man, woman and child – the
  latter a poignant recognition of child mortality.
  Most commentaries on this card refer to the
  archangel as Michael rather than Gabriel.

• The Aleister Crowley Thoth version, which
  changes the title from "Judgment" to "Aeon",
  makes ambiguous allusion to the Egyptian
  deities Horus and Nut.

xx – *Judgment*

Starting-points

• The test of all our learning
• Are we fully alive and
  awake – or do we inhabit
  a living grave?
• Evaluation leading to
  deeper wisdom
• Looking back at the past
  to assess the distance
  travelled and forward to
  assess the way ahead
• What is the all-seeing eye
  that judges us?

XXI – The *World*

The Fool who originally set out on his journey has reached his destination. He has travelled far and learnt a great deal, but where has he arrived? The final card of the Major Arcana, the World, is the supreme symbol of unity, of wholeness. The opposites are reconciled, the material and the spiritual worlds are now experienced as expressions of the same reality, the one a pathway to the other. This is the perfect integration of self and cosmos, the absolute symbol of unity, harmony and balance.

The traveller realizes that what was seen as naïvety, an idealistic dream that separated him from his fellows, was in fact the beginning of wisdom, and the promise of this wisdom has now been fulfilled.

Such profound truths can only be expressed through profound symbols. Hence, the World, with its inexhaustible layers of meaning. The naked, dancing woman, encircled by the laurel wreath of victory, holds the Magician's wand, which has now worked its ultimate magic of self-transformation. At the corners of the card are the four creatures of Ezekiel, representing the four essential qualities: humanity, spirituality, courage and strength. The card's number, twenty-one, is the number of completion (three times seven, the two most magically complete numbers). The wreath also represents zero, symbol of infinity, with which the journey began. The end of one journey marks the start of another.

XXI – The World

Keywords

Destination

Balance

Wholeness

Integration

Self / Cosmos

Completion

Diversity / Unity

The World: in detail

Laurel wreath: The laurel wreath of victory encompasses the complete person and the magic she has at her disposal: it is not a trophy in recognition of specific, worldly attainments. Laurel is also an emblem of peace, purification, protection, divination, secret knowledge and immortality.

Divine gifts: At the four corners of the card are a lion, a bull, a man and an eagle. Ezekiel had a vision of these creatures, in winged form, around God's throne. In Christian symbolism they denote the four evangelists. Their many connotations include diversity in unity, as well as nature within the framework of the divine.

Semi-naked woman: By this stage in the journey physical gender is not significant. We are in the world of higher truth, in which universal values can take female form. This is the unconscious made conscious, first seen in the High Priestess.

Wand: The woman holds the wand that we saw in the hand of the Magician (pages 54–7). Transformation has taken place, and will continue. The magic has been accomplished – but not exhausted.

Variations

- Early Italian decks sometimes show a scene with various buildings, all within a circle to represent the world. In one of the Visconti decks a woman in luxurious clothing floats above a circular panorama of this kind.

- Some historic decks show the central figure as Christ or else the Greek god Hermes (whose name, from which "hermetic" is derived, suggests secret rites and esoteric knowledge).

- In the Rider-Waite version the woman holds a wand in each hand and dances in mid-air. All the basic features here were shown centuries earlier in the Tarot de Marseille. Waite describes the dance as "the swirl of the sensitive life, of joy attained in the body, of the soul's intoxication in the earthly paradise, but still guarded by the Divine Watchers, as if by the powers and the graces of the Holy Name, Tetragammaton, JVHV – those four ineffable letters . . . attributed to the mystical beasts."

XXI – The *World*

Starting-points

- The reconciliation of all opposites
- The wisdom that defies description – with countless levels of meaning
- The mystic dance of creation and harmony
- The secret of happiness
- Qualities that matter most on life's journey
- In our end is our beginning

The Minor Arcana

The Minor Arcana look familiar to us, owing to their similarity to playing cards. There are four suits, each containing ten pip cards plus court cards. Even the names of the Minor Arcana suits appear related to the standard card deck, with pentacles akin to diamonds, cups to hearts, swords to spades and wands to clubs. It is probable that the Minor Arcana derived from the same source as playing cards. Yet in Rider-Waite and many other decks, the numerical symbolism is enriched by a pictorial symbolism that gives added depth.

Introduction

The Minor Arcana have four court cards in each suit rather than the three that are found in modern playing cards, but this seems only a minor difference. If the fourth court card is discarded, all modern card games can be played with the Minor Arcana.

Many people believe that modern playing cards evolved from the Minor Arcana, but more probably the two decks developed independently of each other, from cards brought to Europe from the Middle East. Since these early cards seem to have had three court cards rather than four, modern playing cards may be more true to the original than the Minor Arcana are. One thing is clear: many different decks, which were apparently used mostly for gaming, were circulating in Europe during the 13th century. We cannot be sure, however, why the Major Arcana were added to the Minor Arcana as a set of trumps some time in the 15th century. Were the Major Arcana invented specifically for this purpose, or was an existing deck incorporated with the Minor Arcana in order to provide them with a set of trumps? The latter scenario is more probable, as the 22 symbols of the Major Arcana bear no obvious relationship to those of the Minor Arcana.

The Power of Numbers

If the Minor Arcana were originally merely a deck of gaming cards, how or why did they acquire a symbolic dimension? The answer is that their symbolic significance lies principally in the age-old power of numbers – in this case, the number four into which the suits and the court cards are divided, and the numbers one to ten of the pip cards. Whether the original authors of the cards were conscious of this significance, or whether an unconscious awareness was at work, is not known. However, the numerical principles upon which Minor Arcana are constructed are the major factor in their suitability not just for gaming but also for aiding our understanding of what makes us who we are. Many Tarot readers use just the Major Arcana in their readings; but many use the Minor Arcana as well.

Material reality is built upon numbers. The relationships between the different constituents of matter, and between time and space themselves, can be expressed mathematically. Mathematics existed from the first nanosecond of the Big Bang. Without the exquisite fine-tuning provided by mathematics, reality would have self-destructed in the first moment of creation. Pythagoras, the great 6th-century BC mathematician, philosopher and astronomer, who developed an elaborate theory of numbers, saw mathematics as being essentially mystical. Numbers have no physical existence, yet they order and control every aspect of the universe. The Minor Arcana, which are created from numbers, embody something of this mystical quality.

Four is the number of the material world. There are four

seasons, four cardinal directions (north, east, south and west), four ancient elements (earth, air, fire and water) and four sides to the square – the complementary opposite of the circle, whose movement and fluidity stand for wholeness and completion.

Each of the numbers one to ten carries its own symbolic meaning, as we shall see. In addition to this there is the overall symbolism of each of the four suits. Combining meanings from these two symbolic repertoires, each card of the Minor Arcana conveys its own unique and complex set of messages.

In addition to the individual numerical values of the pip cards, odd numbers, which are inherently unstable, are identified with restlessness, dynamism, movement and achievement; while even numbers, which are stable, are identified with balance and harmony. On the strength of these diverse qualities, odd numbers are traditionally regarded as male and even numbers are regarded as female; odd numbers are seen as the forces that initiate activity and creativity, and even numbers as the forces that give this activity and creativity form and substance.

These various distinctions between odd and even numbers do not imply any kind of priority of one over the other. Odd numbers and even numbers are of equal mathematical and symbolic value. Neither could function mathematically or symbolically without the other. At all points they are complementary, each giving life to the other and arising from the same fundamental source.

Working with the Minor Arcana

Whereas the Major Arcana are concerned primarily with the inner world, the Minor Arcana are more focused on the outer world, on the journey of a material existence in the here and now. They are about our circumstances and our responses to those circumstances, rather than about the deeper questions of an examined life.

When you work with the Minor Arcana, the symbolic meaning of each card is best regarded as representing an aspect of your own psychological nature. Let each card prompt you to look more closely at your character and your emotions. As with the Major Arcana, the cards are to be seen primarily as a form of projective technique, a kind of screen onto which we consciously or unconsciously project (and thus bring to our own attention) our anxieties and aspirations, our ideas about ourselves and others, our hopes and disappointments, our ideals and confusions, and even our long-forgotten dreams and memories.

In many ways this process is even more helpful and revealing than talking to a psychological counsellor or therapist, as there is less tendency to hold back or censor what comes to light. As some of the material uncovered will probably come from the unconscious, we can use the Minor Arcana to gain important insights into ourselves.

Cards of the Minor Arcana

The Minor Arcana are more enigmatic than the Major Arcana in that the meaning of each card does not necessarily strike us so directly. Some cards may even seem to raise more questions than answers, particularly in the case of the pip cards. Yet the Minor Arcana have much to teach us.

The Pip Cards

The number one is the source of harmony and unity, the first manifestation of the Absolute in the physical world. It is the unity to which the multiplicity and diversity of the world will one day return. In the Tarot, the *one* or ace is primary among the pip cards. *Two* is the number of duality, of the twin forces created by the first cause to populate the world; it is man and woman, the primary pair of opposites that is essential for creation but paradoxically has led to the strife and dissent that can destroy creation. *Three* is the Holy Trinity; birth, life and death; past, present and future; body, mind and soul; activity, progress and energy. *Four* is stability and balance, as well as the number of the material world. *Five* is the number of man with his head and four limbs, of the pentacle, of the hand with its five fingers and creative power. *Six* is the six-pointed star, the Seal of Solomon that unites the upward-pointing triangle of matter reaching up to the spiritual world and the downward-pointing triangle of the spiritual world reaching down to matter. *Seven* is the sacred number, the union of

Eight of Cups

first seven numbers have been safely negotiated. *Nine* is the indestructible number, as all its multiples have digits that add up to nine; it therefore signifies the eternal life of the soul when it reaches Paradise. *Ten* is the number of completion, of the One and the Zero placed together, of the First Cause and the Absolute.

The Court Cards

In many Tarot decks the four court cards consist of three male figures (King, Prince, and Page or Knight) and one female (the Queen). This was the pattern established by early decks since it reflected the power distribution of the medieval court, but this imbalance between the sexes robs the Minor Arcana of much of their potential meaning.

the three of the Holy Trinity with the four of the material world, and thus the union of heaven and earth. *Eight* is the number of the initiate, the union of the two circles of infinity, the number of regeneration and resurrection, of the Paradise that is reached when the levels symbolized by the

The four court cards are best seen as reflecting the balanced symbolism seen in the four suits. It is possible that in early decks the Page was intended to suggest a female element, as pages were often androgynous. In many modern decks, though, the fourth court card appears as the Princess, which allows the court cards to represent the four-fold archetypal meaning underpinning the Minor Arcana.

Traditionally the Page (now the Princess) represents the body, the Prince the mind, the Queen the soul and the King the spirit. However, all four images can be aspects of the same reality, an aware and immortal self abiding within a physical body. They can be seen as four stages of life from childhood through adolescence to early and late adulthood. Or they can be seen as the path from potential to realization. At a more complex level, all four cards can be seen as representing different aspects of the same quality – for example, the different stages of innocence in life, from the purity of childhood to the realization in later years that the beginning of all knowledge stems from an understanding of our own ignorance.

Each of the court cards carries a personal meaning depending on its suit, as well as sharing a common archetype represented by its royal rank – with appropriate strengths and weaknesses.

The most mysterious of the court cards, the *Princess* symbolizes the beautiful young woman with her knowledge of secret things. She suggests the source of our intuitive wisdom and of much of our creative genius. At the same time she is elusive and provocative – sometimes accessible, sometimes hidden. She also represents the body, which can work with the mind or at times can refuse to cooperate. In the Princess we can also find the archetype of the trickster who appears as the joker in modern playing cards – someone who disturbs the plans of others and helps us to recognize our own foolishness.

The *Prince* is the archetype of courage, of the hero to whom life is a sacred quest for the magical talisman that will right all wrongs. Noble and upright, he can also be egotistical and headstrong. He can be the inspired leader, but he is capable of becoming withdrawn, isolated or aloof.

The *Queen* personifies the archetype of the mother, who knows the secret of bringing life into the world, who nurtures and protects her children, but who can also become possessive and demanding. She speaks to us of the soul, too, the divine spark that animates the physical body and gives it the potential for greatness.

The *King* is the archetype of the strong, wise sovereign, loved and served by his people. The ruler of all things, he also has connotations of the spirit: he is the representative of the Creator on earth. But he can become authoritarian, even tyrannical, losing touch with his subjects and perhaps becoming remote and inaccessible.

One of Wands

One of Wands

Element: Air

Personality: Male

Values: Potency, inventiveness

One – The Ace, the principal pip card, unity, wholeness, new beginnings, the sum of all possibilities, the Centre, the only indivisible number.

Wands – Element air, colour red, direction east. Male, the sign of the magician, of shape-changing, of growth.

This card with its single wand symbolizes beginnings. It is a symbol of masculine creativity and of the magical power of the male. But this is also the magician's wand, with its power to transform. It invites us to think of the things we would like to change, but it also reminds us to be careful: there could be dangers involved in receiving the changes we wish for.

Two of Wands

Two of Wands

Element: Air

Personality: Male

Values: Ideas, generation

Two – The number of duality, two realizes the new beginnings associated with one. The unity of one becomes the diversity of two.

Wands – Element air, colour red, direction east. Male, the sign of the magician, of shape-changing, of growth.

The two wands of this card come together, supporting each other, but we must remember that as soon as one becomes two, the possibility of conflict arises. The power of combination is ambivalent. Rub two sticks together and we get fire, which may be creative warmth or, alternatively, wasteful destruction. Even conflict can be positive, when it brings clarification and progress.

149

Three of Wands

Three of Wands

Element: Air

Personality: Male

Values: Growth, progress

Three – A sacred number, the number of the Trinity, of heaven; the triangle that points us toward heaven while its base remains on the earth.

Wands – Element air, colour red, direction east. Male, the sign of the magician, of shape-changing, of growth.

The wands are arranged to remind us of the male power of three. The elevated central wand represents the strength of all odd numbers, which, when divided by even numbers, always leave a remainder. Another interpretation is that the Three of Wands represents the initial creative cause (Brahma); yet another view sees it as the soul body that leaves us at death.

Four *of* Wands

Four of Wands

Element: Air

Personality: Male

Values: Thought, idealism

Four – The number of the earth, of the square, of stability. Four brings structure and balance to the dynamic instability of three.

Wands – Element air, colour red, direction east. Male, the sign of the magician, of shape-changing, of growth.

This card emphasizes that four combines the unity of one and the diversity of three. There is also a suggestion of the strength of wands when they are gathered together: one wand can be easily broken, but in a bundle they are unbreakable. We are reminded of the versatile, shape-changing nature of wands. At yet another level, this card conjures up abstract thought, creativity and idealism.

Five of Wands

Five of Wands

Element: Air

Personality: Male

Values: Adventure, experiment

Five – The number of the body and of the hand. Like man, five is inherently unstable unless the extra pip is stabilized by the other four.

Wands – Element air, colour red, direction east. Male, the sign of the magician, of shape-changing, of growth.

The Five of Wands symbolizes an element of risk – perhaps with a touch of excitement. In this depiction the five wands are not carefully balanced: they require a protective mantle to keep them upright and in place. Poised between earth and sky, they are out of touch with each other, thus sacrificing their strength. Are we out of touch with other people, with our life goals, with ourselves?

Six of Wands

Six of Wands

Element: Air

Personality: Male

Values: Projects, ambition

Six – The number of good fortune, of success, of perfect balance. The number of the cube, which faces in all directions and, even when toppled, retains its shape.

Wands – Element air, colour red, direction east. Male, the sign of the magician, of shape-changing, of growth.

The Six of Wands symbolizes the possibility of good fortune in our creative endeavours. Our striving may take us higher than we ever expected. A glorious blossoming may follow. In this particular design, the wands form a triumphal arch, its apex reaching up to the sun; while the shape symbolizes hands that pray for good fortune and protection.

153

Seven *of* Wands

Seven *of* Wands

Element: Air

Personality: Male

Values: Psychic powers, transformation

Seven – Another mystical number, symbolizing the mystery of the sacred. The number of creation that unites the three of heaven with the four of the earth.

Wands – Element air, colour red, direction east. Male, the sign of the magician, of shape-changing, of growth.

This card symbolizes the eternal truth that three supports four, the earth depends upon the heavens: "as above, so below". The earth, the microcosm, is a copy of the heavens, the macrocosm; but it is an imperfect copy. In what ways might the earth be flawed? Perhaps we can acknowledge our worldly failings while at the same time recognizing our hidden talents?

Eight of Wands

Eight of Wands

Eight – Perfect harmony, zero balanced upon zero, without beginning and without end. This is the number of the initiate, of realization.

Wands – Element air, colour red, direction east. Male, the sign of the magician, of shape-changing, of growth.

This card symbolizes the personal strength that comes from recognizing our true nature. Have we learned to trust our powers of insight? If so, we may be entering a new phase of self-understanding. In this design, the circular treetops emphasize that eight is formed from two zeros; the wands below are bursting into flower, which suggests realization.

Element: Air

Personality: Male

Values: Self-knowledge, realism

Nine of Wands

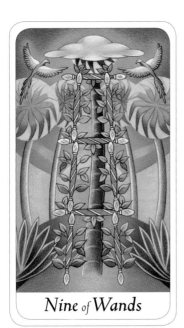

Nine of Wands

Element: Air

Personality: Male

Values: Persistence, effort

Nine – Like three and seven, a particularly sacred number, the product of three times three. Indestructibility, the number of eternity and immortality.

Wands – Element air, colour red, direction east. Male, the sign of the magician, of shape-changing, of growth.

The Nine of Wands has echoes of the Eight, but implies a stronger sense of our own destiny. We are beginning to glimpse more important truths about our possibilities on this earth. In this particular design, the wands are now reaching higher, their apex touching a cloud; the initiate can now see through this cloud and recognize some of what it conceals.

Ten of Wands

Ten of Wands

Element: Air

Personality: Male

Values: Integrity, perfectionism

Ten – The number of completion, formed from the symbols for the number one and for zero. The final stage of the journey through the Minor Arcana.

Wands – Element air, colour red, direction east. Male, the sign of the magician, of shape-changing, of growth.

The Ten of Wands suggest the full flowering of realization. The goal has been reached, what was hidden has become visible. Ten unites all previous numbers in a state of perfect balance. Formed by two groups of five, the number of the hand, it also demonstrates that when two hands are in harmony, the element of risk associated with five is transcended.

Princess of Wands

Princess of Wands

Element: Air

Personality: Male

Values: Intelligence, sincerity

Princess – The ideal of aesthetic beauty, the mistress of earth magic and mysteries, but inclined to be dreamy, lost in imagination and fantasy. Symbol of the body.

Wands – Element air, colour red, direction east. Male, the sign of the magician, of shape-changing, of growth.

The card shows the Princess in her nurturing role, sincere and honest in all she does. As a symbol of the East, she represents the first light of dawn, and her association with the air links her to inspiration, new ideas and new initiatives. But she can be wayward at times, filling us with brilliant, impracticable ideas. Are her feet firmly on the ground? If not, does this matter?

Prince of Wands

Prince of Wands

Element: Air

Personality: Male

Values: Courage, commitment

Prince – The hero archetype, courageous and gifted, but one who risks becoming headstrong and losing his way in his quest for wisdom. The symbol of the mind.

Wands – Element air, colour red, direction east. Male, the sign of the magician, of shape-changing, of growth.

In this card the Prince senses danger. He is uncertain of his path and holds his wand for protection. He reminds us of his nobility and of the sublime vision that always seeks to go beyond the known in its search for truth and greater understanding. How broad are our own horizons in comparison? Do we share something of his vision and commitment to the quest?

Queen of Wands

Queen of Wands

Element: Air

Personality: Male

Values: Nurture, correctness

Queen – The Mother Archetype, but more possessive, controlling and demanding than the Major Arcana Empress. At her best, she represents the soul.

Wands – Element air, colour red, direction east. Male, the sign of the magician, of shape-changing, of growth.

The Queen of Wands is a magical and kindly figure. Of the four elements, air is the most essential for life, and the Queen of Wands is thus the most nurturing of the Queens, although her nurture can at times seem cold and impersonal. She is the most honest of the Queens. In this depiction, the Unicorn is the lunar feminine principle, and otherworldly power.

King *of* Wands

King *of* Wands

Element: Air

Personality: Male

Values: Nobility, power

King – Archetypal male ruler, paternal authority. Echoes the Major Arcana Emperor, but in a weaker, more human form. At his finest, he represents the Spirit.

Wands – Element air, colour red, direction east. Male, the sign of the magician, of shape-changing, of growth.

This card shows the energy of the air at its most potent – although the King of Wands can be wilful, unpredictable and potentially destructive, and inclined to ignore the wishes of mortals. He exemplifies the all-pervasive, ever-present Spirit. Is he also warning us not to become too headstrong and lose touch with others, or not to develop delusions of superiority?

One of Cups

One of Cups

Element: Water

Personality: Female

Values: Talent, harmony

One – The Ace, the principal pip card, unity, wholeness, new beginnings, the sum of all possibilities, the Centre, the only indivisible number.

Cups – Element water, colour blue, direction west. Female, the sign of fertility and nurture, the unconscious, intuitive knowledge, beauty, symmetry, mystery.

This card symbolizes the universal fountain of life, the living water on which all beings depend. There is also a hint of the pestle and mortar (to the ancients a lunar symbol standing for the Great Mother). Other associations include universal love, harmony and peace, together with creativity, beauty and the mystery of the unconscious.

Two of Cups

Two of Cups

Element: Water

Personality: Female

Values: Settlement, sharing

Two – The number of duality, two realizes the new beginnings associated with one. The unity of one becomes the diversity of two.

Cups – Element water, colour blue, direction west. Female, the sign of fertility and nurture, the unconscious, intuitive knowledge, beauty, symmetry, mystery.

This card recalls a key teaching: "The one becomes two and the two give birth to the ten thousand things." One provides the earth with fertility, two actualizes the potential of this fertility. We think of Adam and Eve, the parents of humankind. Here are two cups and two chairs at the table. If the house denotes shelter and safety, do we have the right to live here?

163

Three of Cups

Three of Cups

Element: Water

Personality: Female

Values: Preservation, abundance

Three – A sacred number, the number of the Trinity, of heaven; the triangle that points us toward heaven, while its base remains on the earth.

Cups – Element water, colour blue, direction west. Female, the sign of fertility and nurture, the unconscious, intuitive knowledge, beauty, symmetry, mystery.

The three cups represent the Holy Trinity, symbolizing in earthly terms father, mother and child. In some legends the first child is a hermaphrodite, both male and female, with the possible implication that all human beings have both sexes within themselves. This card has also been taken to symbolize Vishnu, the Preserver.

Four of Cups

Four of Cups

Element: Water

Personality: Female

Values: Enterprise, depth

Four – The number of the earth, of the square, of stability. Four brings structure and balance to the dynamic instability of three.

Cups – Element water, colour blue, direction west. Female, the sign of fertility and nurture, the unconscious, intuitive knowledge, beauty, symmetry, mystery.

Four is the number of the earth, and the ships in this design symbolize that life is now reaching out to the wider world. This is a card of movement, at a steady, ordered pace, as signified by the stability of the number four. The ocean formed by the streams of living water beckons and invites exploration and discovery. What must we do to widen our horizons?

Five of Cups

Five of Cups

Element: Water

Personality: Female

Values: Exploration, mystery

Five – The number of the body and of the hand. Like man, five is inherently unstable unless the extra pip is stabilized by the other four.

Cups – Element water, colour blue, direction west. Female, the sign of fertility and nurture, the unconscious, intuitive knowledge, beauty, symmetry, mystery.

The five cups are harmoniously balanced. Five channels its restless energy into creation. Two of the cups contain something sweet, two hold something bitter. But the fifth cup is a mystery: is it bitter or sweet? In this design, evening sunlight floods through a doorway, reminding us of the Isles of the Blessed that in legend lie beyond the sea to the west.

Six of Cups

Six of Cups

Element: Water

Personality: Female

Values: Optimism, pleasure

Six – The number of good fortune, of success, of perfect balance. The number of the cube, which faces in all directions and, even when toppled, retains its shape.

Cups – Element water, colour blue, direction west. Female, the sign of fertility and nurture, the unconscious, intuitive knowledge, beauty, symmetry, mystery.

The Six of Cups illustrates the balance of the number six, with three cups on either side. It is formed by two sets of three, the number of the Trinity. Perhaps akin to the six found on dice, with the cup openings suggesting the six little depressions, this is a lucky card, but more importantly conjures up joy and optimism.

167

Seven of Cups

Seven of Cups

Element: Water

Personality: Female

Values: Concealment, discretion

Seven – Another mystical number, symbolizing the mystery of the sacred. The number of creation that unites the three of heaven with the four of the earth.

Cups – Element water, colour blue, direction west. Female, the sign of fertility and nurture, the unconscious, intuitive knowledge, beauty, symmetry, mystery.

This card suggests the cups used by a magician to reveal his magical objects. It symbolizes the esoteric, the art of concealment, the mystery that does not meet the eye. Here, four of the cups remain on the quayside, the other three appear on the ship's sails, emphasizing that seven is made up of the three of heaven and the four of earth.

Eight of Cups

Eight of Cups

Element: Water

Personality: Female

Values: Tranquillity, generosity

Eight – Perfect harmony, zero balanced upon zero, without beginning and end. The number of the initiate, of realization.

Cups – Element water, colour blue, direction west. Female, the sign of fertility and nurture, the unconscious, intuitive knowledge, beauty, symmetry, mystery.

Eight is the number of the initiate, of an inner dawning. We need to ask ourselves, how far have we progressed? Have we reached the point of better understanding? Do we recognize the generosity that has been shown to us and the peace from which it stems? In this design, each of the arched openings holds a cup: something has been completed. But what is it?

Nine of Cups

Nine of Cups

Element: Water

Personality: Female

Values: Clarity, exchange

Nine – Like three and seven, a particularly sacred number, the product of three times three. Indestructibility, the number of eternity and immortality.

Cups – Element water, colour blue, direction west. Female, the sign of fertility and nurture, the unconscious, intuitive knowledge, beauty, symmetry, mystery.

This is a card of communication. It suggests the creative stream of ideas, of the arts and sciences, of wisdom and knowledge. The secrets learned in initiation are being shared. The ego that would keep these secrets to itself is transcended. In this version, each cup receives water from one neighbour and gives to another.

Ten of Cups

Ten of Cups

Element: Water

Personality: Female

Values: Selflessness, vision

Ten – The number of completion, formed from the symbols for one and for zero. The final stage of the journey through the Minor Arcana.

Cups – Element water, colour blue, direction west. Female, the sign of fertility and nurture, the unconscious, intuitive knowledge, beauty, symmetry, mystery.

The Ten of Cups asks what we are putting into life and whether that input balances what we are taking out. Willingly and gladly each of the cups pours out its life-giving streams into the world. The card represents the selflessness of all good men and women, whose life-enhancing wish is to enrich the lives of others and to make the world a better place.

171

Princess *of* Cups

Princess *of* Cups

Element: Water

Personality: Female

Values: Spontaneity, beauty

Princess – The ideal of aesthetic beauty, the mistress of earth magic and mysteries, but inclined to be dreamy, lost in imagination and fantasy. Symbol of the body.

Cups – Element water, colour blue, direction west. Female, the sign of fertility and nurture, the unconscious, intuitive knowledge, beauty, symmetry, mystery.

This card shows the most enchanting of the princesses, reminding us that water is free to go where it wills, and is always beautiful. Representing naturalness, generosity, creativity, she questions how well we use such gifts. Here she rides naked on a dolphin – saviour of the shipwrecked, guide to wandering souls.

172

Prince of Cups

Prince of Cups

Element: Water

Personality: Female

Values: Support, encouragement

Prince – The hero archetype, courageous and gifted, but one who risks becoming headstrong and losing his way in his quest for wisdom. The symbol of the mind.

Cups – Element water, colour blue, direction west. Female, the sign of fertility and nurture, the unconscious, intuitive knowledge, beauty, symmetry, mystery.

This Prince acts with intuitive thoughtfulness. A lateral thinker, he often does the unexpected. He seems to have our best interests at heart, and any mistakes are well-intentioned. Here he shows his caring nature by watering his horse before he drinks from his own cup. He gazes into the unconscious, unafraid of what he might find.

173

Queen of Cups

Queen of Cups

Element: Water

Personality: Female

Values: Reflectiveness, stillness

Queen – The Mother Archetype, but more possessive, controlling and demanding than the Major Arcana Empress. At her best, she represents the soul.

Cups – Element water, colour blue, direction west. Female, the sign of fertility and nurture, the unconscious, intuitive knowledge, beauty, symmetry, mystery.

The Queen of Cups is a symbol of peace, quiet waters and the dream world of the unconscious. She conjures up the maternal embrace of warm seas, although her ever-changing nature means that she may become unaware of her children's needs, and turn her embrace to ice. Her stillness never quite becomes inertia.

King of Cups

King of Cups

Element: Water

Personality: Female

Values: Confidence, versatility

King – Archetypal male ruler, paternal authority. Echoes the Major Arcana Emperor, but in a weaker, more human form. At his finest, he represents the spirit.

Cups – Element water, colour blue, direction west. Female, the sign of fertility and nurture, the unconscious, intuitive knowledge, beauty, symmetry, mystery.

The King of Cups is the archetype of sea power, Poseidon to the Greeks, Neptune to the Romans. Representing the Spirit of the Deep he is unfathomable, a guardian of secrets. He rides his white horse in triumph, but is inclined to be impulsive and unpredictable. His trident, crowned with cups, represents the sea's fertility.

175

One *of* Swords

One *of* Swords

Element: Fire

Personality: Male

Values: Concentration, determination

One – The Ace, the principal pip card, unity, wholeness, new beginnings, the sum of all possibilities, the Centre, the only indivisible number.

Swords – Element fire, colour yellow, direction south. Male, the sign of rational thinking, and of the warrior who defeats all obstacles.

A warrior needs only a single sword to cut through confusion and get straight to the heart of any issue or difficulty – by rational, linear thinking. He may need to act alone, with single-minded determination. His loneliness is emphasized in this design by the closed door of the castle. Before entering the castle, the warrior must prove himself.

Two *of* Swords

Two of Swords

Element: Fire

Personality: Male

Values: Cooperation, comradeship

Two – The number of duality, two realizes the new beginnings associated with one. The unity of one becomes the diversity of two.

Swords – Element fire, colour yellow, direction south. Male, the sign of rational thinking, and of the warrior who defeats all obstacles.

The two swords of this card signify companionship, the beginnings of a group of warriors who might one day become an army. This suggests we question our own powers of cooperation, both with others and among our own abilities. When facing a task, are we single-minded, or do the various sides of our nature pull in different directions? This design shows an open landscape, full of possibilities.

Three *of* Swords

Three of Swords

Element: Fire

Personality: Male

Values: Aspiration, leadership

Three – A sacred number, the number of the Trinity, of heaven; the triangle that points us toward heaven, while its base remains on the earth.

Swords – Element fire, colour yellow, direction south. Male, the sign of rational thinking, and of the warrior who defeats all obstacles.

Three swords can form a upward-pointing triangle, reminding us of striving and aspiration. Clarity of leadership is essential, particularly if we have responsibility for others. Note, in this design, that we are once again outside the closed door of the castle: is it clear what we are striving for? Another possible meaning of this card is Shiva, the Agent of Change.

Four *of* Swords

Four of Swords

Element: Fire

Personality: Male

Values: Dynamism, stability

Four – The number of the earth, of the square, of stability. Four brings structure and balance to the dynamic instability of three.

Swords – Element fire, colour yellow, direction south. Male, the sign of rational thinking, and of the warrior who defeats all obstacles.

Four swords can be arranged as a rectangle, symbolizing balance and strength, and harmony among the four essential qualities of this suit: energy, engagement with the world, determination and logical thinking. Here the swords are also arranged to suggest movement between them – stressing that each of these qualities needs to be in constant communication with the others.

179

Five *of* Swords

Five of Swords

Element: Fire

Personality: Male

Values: Unanimity, protection

Five – The number of the body and of the hand. Like man, five is inherently unstable unless the extra pip is stabilized by the other four.

Swords – Element fire, colour yellow, direction south. Male, the sign of rational thinking, and of the warrior who defeats all obstacles.

All five swords pointing skyward show us that it is possible to clarify and direct the aspirations of the Three of Swords. Despite its inherently unstable, risky nature, five is a dynamic number. But care is needed, as there is plenty of scope for discord. We need to be conscious of the possibility of danger. And perhaps we need to ensure that we are sufficiently protected against harm.

Six of Swords

Six of Swords

Element: Fire

Personality: Male

Values: Watchfulness, experience

Six – The number of good fortune, of success, of perfect balance. The number of the cube, which faces in all directions and, even when toppled, retains its shape.

Swords – Element fire, colour yellow, direction south. Male, the sign of rational thinking, and of the warrior who defeats all obstacles.

This is a card that shows achievement. A battle has been won, and victory can be celebrated (note the sword elevated skyward in triumph) – so long as we are sure that we have not fallen prey to self-delusion. Here, the sword in the ground may suggest disappointment. Failure can turn out to be success, but success can also turn out to be failure.

181

Seven *of* Swords

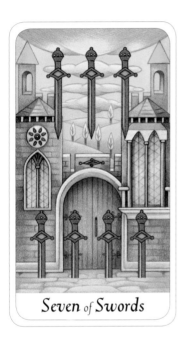

Seven *of* Swords

Seven – Another mystical number, symbolizing the mystery of the sacred. The number of creation that unites the three of heaven with the four of the earth.

Swords – Element fire, colour yellow, direction south. Male, the sign of rational thinking, and of the warrior who defeats all obstacles.

The Seven of Swords signifies the cutting of a cord to realize the true potential of ourselves or of a situation. This may require us to prioritize, or to separate issues that might otherwise become entangled. The higher purpose may not be easy to discern when lower aspirations are also clamouring for our attention. Somehow we may need to serve both.

Element: Fire

Personality: Male

Values: Perspective, coordination

Eight of Swords

Eight of Swords

Element: Fire

Personality: Male

Values: Expertise, welcome

Eight – Perfect harmony, zero balanced upon zero, without beginning and without end. This is the number of the initiate, of realization.

Swords – Element fire, colour yellow, direction south. Male, the sign of rational thinking, and of the warrior who defeats all obstacles.

Eight is the number of the initiate: entry into the castle has now been granted. Initiation implies that a test has been successfully completed, and new opportunities have opened up. We can count ourselves among a new set of peers. We also have new skills. But self-examination will be needed to discover what they are and how best to put them into practice.

Nine of Swords

Nine of Swords

Element: Fire

Personality: Male

Values: Learning, dignity

Nine – Like three and seven, a particularly sacred number, the product of three times three. Indestructibility, the number of eternity and immortality.

Swords – Element fire, colour yellow, direction south. Male, the sign of rational thinking, and of the warrior who defeats all obstacles.

The Nine of Swords is a reminder that time passes swiftly. How do we deal with this? Perhaps what has been learned cannot easily be forgotten, and our capacities grow with our experience. Or we may be leaving things too late, or missing our opportunities. This design shows one sword apart, reminding us that, like the warrior, we are essentially alone in our quest.

Ten of Swords

Ten of Swords

Element: Fire

Personality: Male

Values: Self-questioning, seniority

Ten – The number of completion, formed from the symbols for one and for zero. The final stage of the journey through the Minor Arcana.

Swords – Element fire, colour yellow, direction south. Male, the sign of rational thinking, and of the warrior who defeats all obstacles.

The Ten of Swords suggests promotion to a new level of operation. Having endured the struggle, we can provide wise counsel. Having fought for our self-respect, we can help others who are less advanced. The card gives reassurance, while still posing questions. Have we fought the right battles in life? Do we deserve the respect that is offered to us by those who lack our experience?

Princess of Swords

Princess of Swords

Element: Fire

Personality: Male

Values: Challenge, passion

Princess – The ideal of aesthetic beauty, the mistress of earth magic and mysteries, but inclined to be dreamy, lost in imagination and fantasy. Symbol of the body.

Swords – Element fire, colour yellow, direction south. Male, the sign of rational thinking, and of the warrior who defeats all obstacles.

The Princess of Swords is the strongest and most warrior-like of the Princesses. She can wound, but also cut through falsehood. Swords are a male sign, and she challenges us with her fiery temperament. The Princess of Swords asks how comfortable we are in the presence of female power, in ourselves or others. Can we accept the Amazon archetype as we accept the Hero?

Prince of Swords

Prince of Swords

Element: Fire

Personality: Male

Values: Caution, deliberation

Prince – The hero archetype, courageous and gifted, but one who risks becoming headstrong and losing his way in his quest for wisdom. The symbol of the mind.

Swords – Element fire, colour yellow, direction south. Male, the sign of rational thinking, and of the warrior who defeats all obstacles.

The Prince of Swords is undecided which path to take: back to the world he knows, symbolizing the mind's comfort zone, or forward into the unknown, symbolizing risky but exciting new ideas? His indecision is not a lack of courage, but uncertainty about new insights, scientific or artistic, that could undermine or destroy much that is familiar to us.

Queen of Swords

Queen of Swords

Element: Fire

Personality: Male

Values: Freedom, artfulness

Queen – The Mother Archetype, but more possessive, controlling and demanding than the Major Arcana Empress. At her best, she represents the soul.

Swords – Element fire, colour yellow, direction south. Male, the sign of rational thinking, and of the warrior who defeats all obstacles.

The Queen of Swords strides toward us, flourishing her sword, intent on cutting through the cords that inhibit or even imprison the true self. At the same time her sword can, like fire, become an agent of discord and destruction. She is the queen of the arts of manipulation, and is not above using people and situations in order to achieve her goals.

King *of* Swords

King *of* Swords

Element: Fire

Personality: Male

Values: Majesty, righteousness

King – Archetypal male ruler, paternal authority. Echoes the Major Arcana Emperor, but in a weaker, more human form. At his finest, he represents the Spirit.

Swords – Element fire, colour yellow, direction south. Male, the sign of rational thinking, and of the warrior who defeats all obstacles.

The King of Swords is the most powerful of the four kings, and symbolizes the determination and energy to sweep impediments aside in the interests of truth and justice. He rides forcefully toward us, defending his kingdom behind him. The passion of the King of Swords can be a force for good but can also manifest itself at times as overreaction and anger.

189

One *of* Pentacles

One *of* Pentacles

Element: Earth

Personality: Female

Values: Enchantment, inclusiveness

One – The Ace, the principal pip card, unity, wholeness, new beginnings, the sum of all possibilities, the Centre, the only indivisible number.

Pentacles – Element earth, colour green, direction north. Female, the sign of nature, of elemental forces, of earth magic, of stardust.

Pentacles are the most mysterious suit, identified with the legendary north, where for the original Tarot authors the green, fertile lands lay. The One suggests enchantment, an ability to absorb and contain the power of others. In this design a tall building unites the earth's darkness and the sun's light, both essential for growth. If the pentacle is seen as a guiding star, where will it lead us?

Two of Pentacles

Two of Pentacles

Element: Earth

Personality: Female

Values: Commemoration, depth

Two – The number of duality, two realizes the new beginnings associated with one. The unity of one becomes the diversity of two.

Pentacles – Element earth, colour green, direction north. Female, the sign of nature, of elemental forces, of earth magic, of stardust.

This card has connotations of equilibrium and harmony. Ideally everything is in balance and will be kept in that state – past and future, memory and hope, sky and earth, privacy and openness. A mysterious light floods the darkness. Now that the one has become two and new beginnings are afoot, endings are also possible. Unless we remember that all created things pass away, we live in only two dimensions.

Three of Pentacles

Three of Pentacles

Element: Earth

Personality: Female

Values: Diversity, wonder

Three – A sacred number, the number of the Trinity, of heaven; the triangle that points us toward heaven, while its base remains on the earth.

Pentacles – Element earth, colour green, direction north. Female, the sign of nature, of elemental forces, of earth magic, of stardust.

In the Three of Pentacles multiplicity becomes life-enhancing, if only we have trained our eyes to appreciate wonder and our heart to revere its spiritual source. The diversity of creation is apparent everywhere – we can even add to it, in our own way. When three stars animate the sky, they imply that earth is also involved in their revelation.

Four of Pentacles

Four of Pentacles

Element: Earth

Personality: Female

Values: Practicality, reliability

Four – The number of the earth, of the square, of stability. Four brings structure and balance to the dynamic instability of three.

Pentacles – Element earth, colour green, direction north. Female, the sign of nature, of elemental forces, of earth magic, of stardust.

Traditionally, the Four of Pentacles symbolizes reliability, good humour, practical wisdom and the physical sciences. Down-to-earth excellence is at work, and it will not fail us if we appreciate both its strengths and limitations. The card also suggests the benevolence of nature, which is capable of supplying much that we will need. A bird can fly through the trees, as well as high in the air.

193

Five of Pentacles

Five of Pentacles

Element: Earth

Personality: Female

Values: Unpredictability, serendipity

Five – The number of the body and of the hand. Like man, five is inherently unstable unless the extra pip is stabilized by the other four.

Pentacles – Element earth, colour green, direction north. Female, the sign of nature, of elemental forces, of earth magic, of stardust.

The Five of Pentacles symbolizes the creative spirit that moves through the natural world – an adventurous approach to life will bring its own good fortune. We should not, however, expect symmetry and neatness. And things can go wrong: nature can become misshapen, and can produce poisons as well as nourishment. There is always a dark side, even in ourselves.

Six of Pentacles

Six of Pentacles

Element: Earth

Personality: Female

Values: Abundance, acceptance

Six – The number of good fortune, of success, of perfect balance. The number of the cube, which faces in all directions and, even when toppled, retains its shape.

Pentacles – Element earth, colour green, direction north. Female, the sign of nature, of elemental forces, of earth magic, of stardust.

The Six of Pentacles tells us that the earth's abundance, although so often available, is not ours to command. We must live in harmony with the earth, not expect the earth to harmonize with us. An over-controlling attitude can be destructive. The two red triangles, one pointing up, and one down, indicate caprice and uncertainty, even within a reliable framework.

195

Seven of Pentacles

Seven of Pentacles

Element: Earth

Personality: Female

Values: Efficiency, self-respect

Seven – Another mystical number, symbolizing the mystery of the sacred. The number of creation that unites the three of heaven with the four of the earth.

Pentacles – Element earth, colour green, direction north. Female, the sign of nature, of elemental forces, of earth magic, of stardust.

Pentacles represent the earth, while seven is the number of creation. Thus, this card symbolizes the six days that brought the world into being, and the seventh day on which God rested. The seventh day, which is held sacred (at the apex in this design), prompts us to give thought to how we use our free time – and our time management in general.

Eight of Pentacles

Eight of Pentacles

Element: Earth

Personality: Female

Values: Sincerity, groundedness

Eight – Perfect harmony, zero balanced upon zero, without beginning and end. The number of the initiate, of realization.

Pentacles – Element earth, colour green, direction north. Female, the sign of nature, of elemental forces, of earth magic, of stardust.

The Eight of Pentacles, which combines eternity with the five-pointed star symbolic of humankind, is the most significant of the Eights, standing for our true nature. Whatever weaknesses we perceive in ourselves, there is potential for perfect harmony if we can attune ourselves to nature – its miracles and its mysteries. How should we initiate ourselves in nature's teachings?

197

Nine of Pentacles

Nine of Pentacles

Element: Earth

Personality: Female

Values: Dedication, foresight

Nine – Like three and seven, a particularly sacred number, the product of three times three. Indestructibility, the number of eternity and immortality.

Pentacles – Element earth, colour green, direction north. Female, the sign of nature, of elemental forces, of earth magic, of stardust.

The Nine of Pentacles represents our innate talents, the gifts we were born with. The card is challenging, for in reminding us of the many opportunities for personal growth it also warns us that it would be folly to neglect those chances. In alliance with nature we can reach attainments of lasting value, and perhaps leave a generous legacy to those who follow in our footsteps.

Ten of Pentacles

Ten of Pentacles

Element: Earth

Personality: Female

Values: Compromise, self-knowledge

Ten – The number of completion, formed from the symbols for one and for zero. The final stage of the journey through the Minor Arcana.

Pentacles – Element earth, colour green, direction north. Female, the sign of nature, of elemental forces, of earth magic, of stardust.

The Ten of Pentacles, which completes the journey, asks us to reflect on what we have learned and ask ourselves whether we have been too demanding in our requirements. There is a place for perfectionism, but it is possible to add one finishing touch too many – to become excessively stressed over tiny details. Are our motives for demanding excellence altruistic or selfish?

Princess of Pentacles

Princess of Pentacles

Element: Earth

Personality: Female

Values: Melody, seclusion

Princess – The ideal of aesthetic beauty, the mistress of earth magic and mysteries, but inclined to be dreamy, lost in imagination and fantasy. Symbol of the body.

Pentacles – Element earth, colour green, direction north. Female, the sign of nature, of elemental forces, of earth magic, of stardust.

The Princess of Pentacles, who represents the beauty of nature, generates a natural music that can have unexpected effects. Full of creative energy, she draws us to fields and woodlands, and to secret places of the landscape, such as copses and groves. If we wish to receive the gifts of the Princess of Pentacles, we must approach her as suitors, not as overlords.

Prince of Pentacles

Prince of Pentacles

Prince – The hero archetype, courageous and gifted, but one who risks becoming headstrong and losing his way in his quest for wisdom. The symbol of the mind.

Pentacles – Element earth, colour green, direction north. Female, the sign of nature, of elemental forces, of earth magic, of stardust.

The Prince of Pentacles is the most assured of the Princes, secure in the power of nature. He is a formidable juggler, someone who keeps diverse elements in a complex balance that may threaten at times to collapse. He is relaxed and outgoing, although highly intelligent. The confidence and showmanship of the Prince of Pentacles can lead him to take serious risks.

Element: Earth

Personality: Female

Values: Confidence, dexterity

Queen of Pentacles

Queen of Pentacles

Element: Earth

Personality: Female

Values: Workmanship, wealth

Queen – The Mother Archetype, but more possessive, controlling and demanding than the Major Arcana Empress. At her best, she represents the soul.

Pentacles – Element earth, colour green, direction north. Female, the sign of nature, of elemental forces, of earth magic, of stardust.

The Queen of Pentacles represents two aspects of spinning: creativity (as in the spinning wheel) and entrapment (as in the spider's web). Nature can be rapacious as well as generous, and brings death as well as life. The Queen of Pentacles is the queen of unlimited natural bounty, but at her worst she can be covetous – attached to luxury and wealth.

King of Pentacles

King of Pentacles

Element: Earth

Personality: Female

Values: Instinct, civilization

King – Archetypal male ruler, paternal authority. Echoes the Major Arcana Emperor, but in a weaker, more human form. At his finest, he represents the Spirit.

Pentacles – Element earth, colour green, direction north. Female, the sign of nature, of elemental forces, of earth magic, of stardust.

The King of Pentacles, who rules the element earth, has a detailed understanding of nature. But he is also the Green Man, amoral ruler of the pagan kingdom of nature spirits and elemental forces. The King of Pentacles warns us of the dangers of seeking to overrule the claims of nature with our man-made sciences. At times spiritual, he seeks control.

203

Working with the Tarot

We all strive to find meaning and purpose in our lives, and the Tarot is a wonderful tool to assist us in this quest. Once you have gained some familiarity with the cards, their archetypes and their multi-layered symbolism, and worked through the meanings of the Major and Minor Arcana in sequence, you are ready to begin further explorations. You might start with meditation, which helps to open your mind further to the significance of the imagery. Then it is worthwhile seeing whether card layouts work for you. Whichever path you choose, do not be tempted to over-intellectualize. Hold the cards in your mind and let meanings spin off naturally.

Meditation

Meditation sounds easy. The idea is simply to become aware of your own mind: surely we do this all the time? Unfortunately, this is not the case. We are usually aware of a swirling swarm of thoughts, but not of the mind that has these thoughts. We rarely stand back and watch our minds. Even more rarely do we empty our minds of thoughts and experience the mind as it actually is, free from the mental chatter that usually dominates our waking life. Meditation is thus, for many people, a completely new experience and one that requires regular practice to master it.

There are many different techniques of meditation, but they have one thing in common: a point of focus on which to concentrate.

This may be visual – which is where the Tarot comes in, as we shall see. But first it might be worthwhile to concentrate on your own physical presence. The breath is the most popular focus, because the breath is always with us. Sit comfortably in a quiet spot and turn your attention to the cool sensation of the air entering your nostrils as you breathe in, and the warmer sensation of the air leaving your nose as you breathe out. When thoughts arise, don't try to push them away; either watch them impersonally or ignore them. Do not become involved in them.

When meditating on the Tarot, first allow your mind to settle into this peaceful state, then transfer your attention from your breath to the card in front of you. Observe it

206

closely, but without the fixed concentration you would use if you were reading a book. Keep your mind open and let the cards speak to you by attending to whatever impressions arise in response to them. Don't try to analyze any of these impressions. The time to ponder on meaning is when the meditation is over. For now, just experience the cards without comment or judgment, rather as you accept images in dreams. Thinking about the cards too much is likely to interrupt the flow.

Later, when you do think about the cards, you may be surprised by the insights they convey. For example, they may bring up things about yourself you did not know, suggestions for resolving problems and difficulties, clues for self-development or spiritual guidance, or they may awaken various feelings from which you can learn. Take this relaxed, open-minded approach whether you choose the cards on which to meditate, draw one at random from a deck, or work with a whole layout as described in the pages that follow.

XVIII – The **Moon**

Readings and Layouts

The main value of the Tarot is that it presents us with a series of symbolic pictures that relate to the universal, archetypal concepts that constitute the inherited part of the unconscious mind. Working with the Tarot cards helps you to access these archetypal energies, and in the process facilitate your psychological and spiritual development. In addition, when using the Tarot cards, we also, often without realizing it, project onto them many of our conscious and unconscious preoccupations, anxieties, wishes, hopes, doubts and psychological complexes. This means that the Tarot can be a highly effective tool for gaining an understanding of what is going on deep within our own minds.

An invaluable method for working with the Tarot is to meditate on the individual cards, using each one as a symbolic signpost on your inner journey. However, you may also like to try arranging the cards in layouts, so that each card can be read in conjunction with those around it, in a way that supplements or modifies its meaning. Taken in its entirety, a layout may provide an overall guide to the inner life. Some people consider, in addition, that the way the cards fall after they are shuffled and laid out is an example of what Jung called synchronicity: a set of meaningful coincidences that cannot be explained as created purely by chance. Those who subscribe to this view believe that, given a sensitive approach to interpretation, there will be a meaningful connection between each card and the others in the layout, and between the cards and events in your own life, whether past, present or future. Others prefer not to read too much into the way the cards arrange themselves, but to focus solely upon their self-contained meanings. Either way, the layouts can assist us toward deeper levels of self-understanding.

You can devise your own layouts if you wish, or simply choose a number that has special meaning for you and lay down an equivalent number of cards. Whatever method you adopt, remember that the interpretation of the cards is dependent upon the symbolism of each of the images, but that it is also bound to be subjective. When working with the same spread of cards, two people are sure to find differences in their interpretation. This is partly, of course, because the cards relate to an individual, whose issues are peculiar to him or herself. The *querent*, or seeker, may or may not be professionally ambitious, or believe in an afterlife, or feel trapped in a relationship, or be seeking an outlet for their creative urges. The cards will yield different meanings according to the individual concerns that we bring to them, and the relative priorities that we attach to those preoccupations.

In addition, we are all different in the way that we use our minds to interpret any situation, and these differences of mental processing also play a part in the responses we will have to a layout – or even to an individual card. Some people are interested in exploring the esoteric symbolism in depth, while others react to the imagery at a more immediate, emotional level. Some people challenge themselves quite deeply in their readings, aiming to understand themselves more thoroughly. Others look for practical solutions to their problems in a spirit of hopeful inquiry, without giving much thought to the question of whether they would benefit from personal transformation. All of these approaches are equally valid. In a sense we each of us have our own special Tarot, that we create for ourselves by usage.

As far as possible, approach the cards with a clear, open mind, as in meditation, and let the symbolism of the cards speak to you. Do not try to shape the meaning to fit your conscious wishes. Let the cards do the work. And if you do find yourself projecting any of your unconscious complexes or concerns onto them, accept and reflect on these, too. They are all part of the process of revelation.

It is good to be as relaxed as possible when you perform a reading for yourself or for a friend. Spend five minutes or so emptying your mind and breathing slowly and deeply. Tune your attention, but without preparing yourself for a great mental effort: you are not sitting an exam! Nor are you solving a puzzle of logic or arithmetic. If you believe that there is a correct answer, you are approaching the cards with the wrong attitude. You are a seeker, and you are grateful for any glimpses of truth the cards may bring you, however those glimpses may originate. An insight that springs suddenly into your mind might be just as valuable as a conclusion that you have worked out by analysis. Take note of your feelings as well as your thoughts. Just let the possible meanings emerge from your encounter with the cards, and if the cards seem to be at odds with each other, try to stay relaxed – life is full of contradictions, so it would not be surprising to find apparent inconsistencies in what the cards are saying to you.

Tarot readings must take into account the fact that the language of symbolism has a vocabulary but no grammar. Imagine that you have drawn the Tower, and the card reminds you that several people have commented on how ambitious you are, even to the point of self-sacrifice. Is such ambition a good or a bad thing? The symbol of the Tower cannot comment on this: it can only serve to trigger your own discovery of the wisest, most useful message that you can derive from its appearance in the layout. Look at the neighbouring cards to see if any of them seem to provide you with a gloss on the Tower – if so, this will be a reflection of your unconscious wisdom, which the Tarot is helping you to source.

Seven-card Horseshoe

Seven, composed of three, the number of heaven, and four, the number of the earth, suggests the blending of higher aspirations with down-to-earth realities. This is the layout often chosen by people who are pondering personal and sometimes practical problems. In this layout the seven cards represent the combined inspiration of heaven and earth, while the horseshoe represents the top curve of a question mark.

Lay out the cards face down and enter a meditative state, then turn up each card in turn, in the sequence shown. Don't hurry: open up to the symbolism before you.

Card One represents the past and the influences upon you that may have a bearing upon the problem.

Card Two represents the present and the psychological and spiritual effects that the problem may be having upon you.

Cards Three and Four symbolize the personal qualities that may help you to resolve the problem.

Cards Five and Six, by contrast, symbolize the qualities that may hinder the resolution.

Card Seven suggests how you might avoid similar problems in the future.

Progressing through the cards in this way allows relevant questions to suggest themselves. These questions may help you to understand the problem's true nature and your relationship to it. They are likely to be the questions a good counsellor would raise – ones that generate

fresh insights. Don't be concerned if nothing comes immediately to mind. Put the cards to one side and allow your unconscious to incubate the experience. Insights may arise spontaneously during the following hours or days. Don't rush to repeat the exercise either. Give incubation a chance to do its work.

The cards are not there to present you with ready-made answers. They are designed to help you to develop your own powers of self-reflection and problem-solving. You already know far more than you think, but much of your knowledge is buried in your unconscious. The cards prompt you to gain access to some of this knowledge, and to recognize how best to apply it.

A variation is the **Five-card Horseshoe**, in which a single card replaces 3 and 4, and 5 and 6.

Celtic Cross

The Celtic Cross combines Christ's cross, symbolizing the descent of the spirit into the physical world, and the circle, signifying heaven, completion and infinity. It is a potent symbol, capable of inspiring insight after insight the more we focus on it in meditation. It is most frequently used when you are dealing with large issues – such as fundamental questions of life's meaning and purpose. The layout does not show the full Celtic Cross, but it suggests it, and the symbolism that the Celtic Cross represents should be held in the mind while working with the layout.

The Celtic Cross differs from the Seven-card Horseshoe in that you start with a card of your choice, one you feel represents the question you wish to ask. Lay this card face up on the table and dwell on its symbolism for a few minutes. Then shuffle the pack and take the top card, laying it face-down to cover your chosen card exactly (1). Lay the next card face-down to cross this one (2). Then arrange the next four cards below, above and to the left and right of the cross (3–6).

Turn up the face-down cards one by one in the sequence shown, contemplating each one in turn.

Card One represents yourself and the general influences upon you that affect the question.

Card Two symbolizes material concerns or obstacles and their relationship to the question.

Card Three portrays the qualities that you have, or need, to answer the question.

Card Four shows the past experiences that may help you with this answer.

Card Five symbolizes the hopes and wishes, and perhaps also the fears, connected with the answer.

Card Six stands for the actions you could take that might help with the answer.

As with all the layouts, do not expect the cards to find the answer for you. The solution lies within yourself and the cards are there to help you access it. Alternatively, if you believe the answer comes from a spiritual source outside yourself, the cards are there to help you open the channel to this source.

Tree of Life

Unlike the Seven-card Horseshoe and the Celtic Cross, the Tree of Life is not designed to assist the seeker with specific questions; rather, it helps with the processes of inner development. It provides you with potential guidance for each of the three paths along which such development takes place: spiritual, intellectual and emotional.

The Tarot Tree of Life must not be confused with the Sephiroth, the symbolic Tree of Life used by students of Kabbalah, the Jewish mystical tradition. There are similarities between the two, but the Tarot Tree is much less complex and much more accessible.

Shuffle the deck, face-down, then lay out eleven cards in three columns, with five cards in the centre and three on each side (see page 219 for an example).

Turn the cards over and meditate on each one in turn, working your way upward from the bottom of the central column, then upward from the bottom of the left-hand column and finally from the bottom of the right-hand column. Each column represents our ascent, our development on the path concerned: the spiritual path in the centre, the intellectual on the left, the emotional on the right.

SPIRITUAL PATH
Card One is physical self-awareness, **Card Two** your awareness of the natural world, **Card Three** your awareness of spiritual realities, **Card Four** your awareness of your own spiritual

nature and **Card Five** your awareness of the divine.

INTELLECTUAL PATH

Card Six is self-knowledge, **Card Seven** self-control and **Card Eight** self-mastery.

EMOTIONAL PATH

Card Nine is compassion, **Card Ten** empathy and **Card Eleven** universal love.

The qualities on each path are arranged in ascending order, in the way they are usually acquired in life. For example, we cannot gain self-control without self-knowledge; and self-mastery is a higher form of self-control. However, we do not progress at the same rate along each path.

We might be empathetic but have an undeveloped awareness of the natural world. We might have an awareness of spiritual realities but be unable to use our mind to control our heart – succumbing to depression or jealousy when disappointed in love.

Once you have looked at each column in turn, consider how the cards interrelate across the columns. The interplay of these three aspects of ourselves must be observed and understood if we are to know ourselves fully. The seven sample Tree of Life readings over the following pages should suggest ways in which this layout can be used. Note that the eleven categories are often interpreted loosely: too rigorous an application of them would be self-defeating.

Tree of Life, Reading 1

The querent is a full-time architect, aged 27, with two children. She wants to be a psychotherapist and is taking a counselling course. Her husband's parents care for the children after school. The querent found this arrangement convenient initially, but now it feels claustrophobic. The grandparents buy the children clothes she dislikes and, while kindly, they are of the "speak when you're spoken to" school of childcare.

SPIRITUAL PATH

1 Physical self-awareness

XII The Hanged Man – Hanging by one leg was once the usual punishment for being in debt and may prompt the querent to consider her own indebtedness, or even guilt. She may feel an obligation to the grandparents and guilt at her own resentment – and her inability to express it. Underlying this is perhaps a desire to spend more time with her children, coupled with anxieties about her career–family imbalance.

2 Awareness of the natural world

XVI The Tower – The Tower can symbolize hopelessness, but also liberation and transformation. The lightning does not destroy the tower, but makes it smaller. Perhaps the querent could work part-time as an architect while gaining experience as a counsellor.

3 Awareness of spiritual realities

VI The Lovers – This card represents two sides of femininity: maiden or seductress, or, in the querent's case, mother or professional woman.

INTELLECTUAL PATH   SPIRITUAL PATH   EMOTIONAL PATH

8
XIX – The Sun

5
XX – Judgment

11
II – The High Priestess

7
X – The Wheel of Fortune

4
XXI – The World

10
I – The Magician

6
XI – Justice

3
VI – The Lovers

9
V – The Hierophant

2
XVI – The Tower

1
XII – The Hanged Man

Physical love can co-exist with motherly nurture. The male suitor points to the role of the querent's husband as supportive partner. How can he help in this situation?

4 Awareness of inner spirit

XXI The World – The wand is a reminder that change lies in our hands. The querent has the right to be her own person and to raise her children as she chooses. The creatures represent humanity, spirituality, courage and strength – tools with which she can guide her in-laws to see her point of view.

5 Awareness of the divine

XX Judgment – This suggests self-scrutiny. If the querent is tempted to criticize her in-laws, she might reflect on her own past choices.

Have these choices contributed to her quandary?

INTELLECTUAL PATH

6 Self-knowledge

XI Justice – Justice wields the sword of truth and the scales that weigh up our actions. Whether the querent's arrangements are right for her in-laws is less crucial than whether they are right for her. Her own approach should be respected.

7 Self-control

X The Wheel of Fortune – This image of the inherent uncertainty of existence can bring up fears of change, but it is a symbol of hope. Is it time for the querent to take control of her future? This may involve changes to her work as well as with her in-laws. Change can be accomplished sensitively if wisdom (the sphinx) presides.

8 Self-mastery

XIX The Sun – An image of creativity, the sun inspires the querent to seek imaginative solutions. When approaching her employers about working part-time, objections are less likely if change is presented positively. Perhaps she could turn freelance to arrange her work to suit herself and her family.

EMOTIONAL PATH
9 Compassion

V The Hierophant – The three supplicants before the high priest may remind the querent that it is not just her own happiness at stake but her whole family's. When she expresses her feelings to her in-laws, she might recall that their original motive was to help her.

10 Empathy

I The Magician – The Magician is the master of transformation, heralding new beginnings. The querent's ability to bring about changes will be enhanced by practising her counselling skills.

11 Love for all creation

II The High Priestess – This is a symbol of female spiritual mastery. Through her studies the querent gains deeper understanding of people. One insight is that most people do the best they can with what they know. The querent can embrace her in-laws' differing outlook non-judgmentally while remaining true to her own attitudes.

Tree of Life, Reading 2

The querent is a single father aged 42 with a 10-year-old son, Jake. He works as a personnel supervisor in a supermarket and played jazz saxophone until Jake's mother, also a keen musician, died of cancer two years ago. The querent no longer has time to play, but to his delight Jake loves music too, showing talent. In accordance with his late wife's wishes, he wants Jake to attend a music school, but cannot afford the fees.

SPIRITUAL PATH

1 Physical self-awareness

I The Magician – The recent loss of Jake's mother is a reminder of our physical mortality. The number one symbolizes the start of a journey and Jake faces a new beginning: next year he moves from primary to secondary school. As the magician in Jake's life, the querent can help him to realize his potential.

2 Awareness of the natural world

IV The Emperor – The Emperor represents creative dynamism and striving, the force of will. This can inspire the querent to pursue all avenues to get Jake into music school: are there scholarships? But emperors must beware of becoming tyrants, so the querent should beware of imposing his own musical aspirations on his son.

3 Awareness of spiritual realities

X The Wheel of Fortune – The Wheel of Fortune can turn our world upside down. In doing all he can to foster Jake's own love of music, he would be honouring his

INTELLECTUAL PATH   SPIRITUAL PATH   EMOTIONAL PATH

8
0 – The Fool

5
XX - Judgment

11
XI - Justice

7
VII – The Chariot

4
XVII – The Star

10
XVI – The Tower

6
III – The Empress

3
X - The Wheel of Fortune

9
XV - The Devil

2
IV - The Emperor

1
I – The Magician

partner's memory – and turning the Wheel of Fortune away from grief toward joy and hope.

4 Awareness of inner spirit

XVII The Star – The woman emptying water into a river recalls the querent's wife, who remains a spiritual presence as the river of life flows onward. More generally, this card points to the care and nurture that parents give their children, preparing them to enter adult life.

5 Awareness of the divine

XX Judgment – The dead rising from their graves at the sound of the trumpet suggests the querent's desire to keep his partner's memory alive through music. The trumpet-playing angel is a reminder of music's uplifting power.

INTELLECTUAL PATH

6 Self-knowledge

III The Empress – The Empress could represent the predominance of the mother in the querent's decision-making. In spite of his desire to honour her wishes, is the music school what he and Jake both truly want? If not, she would probably have respected his honesty. The Empress, after all, is the guardian of truth.

7 Self-control

VII The Chariot – The two horses, apparently pulling different ways, represent the choices faced by a single parent attempting to steer a steady path through life. The card reminds the querent that he should not be afraid to explore new directions by applying for a better-paid job or opportunities to earn extra money through his own musical talent.

8 Self-mastery

0 The Fool – The Fool is widely understood as the self, beginning life's journey as an innocent, on the way to attaining wisdom. The querent must think of the future: what is his goal in sending Jake to music school? Does he hope Jake will become a professional musician? Does Jake himself share that ambition?

EMOTIONAL PATH

9 Compassion

XV The Devil – The tempter Satan represents the tests we face on the path to fulfilment. Following the questions raised by the Fool, this card reinforces the querent's need to be certain to consider his son's own desires.

10 Empathy

XVI The Tower – The lightning bolt shakes the foundations of the ego, to bring enlightenment (the sun) and liberation from pride. Has the querent's pride prevented him from asking family members for assistance, even financial? He may be surprised at their generosity.

11 Love for all creation

XI Justice – The sword denotes truth – perhaps the fact that music is central to the querent's life. Justice shows him that he can find a balance between music, money and memory that honours himself, his son and his late partner.

Tree of Life, Reading 3

The querent is a student, aged 18, who lives with her doctor parents and 16-year-old brother in an urban environment. They are a close-knit family. Next term she is due to begin a medical degree 200 miles away. A lover of fashion, she dreams of running her own fashion business, but has always regarded this as an unrealistic fantasy. Until last week, that is. On her 18th birthday, she bought her first lottery ticket "for a laugh" – and won three million.

SPIRITUAL PATH

1 Physical self-awareness

XIV Temperance – The angelic figure pours water from the vessel of the spirit into the vessel of the earthly realm. The opportunities offered to the querent by her sudden wealth are overwhelming, but she should try to remain grounded. Meditation may help.

2 Awareness of the natural world

XVIII The Moon – The moon is often linked with the feminine and with the unconscious. The crayfish suggests the querent's inner conflict. To gain perspective, perhaps she would benefit from a break from her environment, such as a period of travel.

3 Awareness of spiritual realities

XXI The World – The last of the Major Arcana, the World represents the end of a journey. For the querent, just 18, it is the journey of childhood, for she is now officially an adult, and

INTELLECTUAL PATH   **SPIRITUAL PATH**   **EMOTIONAL PATH**

8
XII - The Hanged Man

5
II - The High Priestess

11
I - The Magician

7
VI - The Lovers

4
IX - The Hermit

10
III - The Empress

6
XIII - Death

3
XXI - The World

9
XI - Justice

2
XVIII - The Moon

1
XIV - Temperance

227

financially independent, too. Her future is in her own hands, but she need not face it alone – she can draw support from her family.

4 Awareness of inner spirit

IX The Hermit – The Hermit symbolizes retreat within ourselves, seeking insight through examining core values. Having won the lottery, the querent may find she attracts attention, some unwelcome. Retaining a sense of herself, she will gain the wisdom to light her path.

5 Awareness of the divine

II The High Priestess – The image of the noble High Priestess brings to mind the lofty path of study. The querent could easily use her win to pursue her dreams in the fashion world; but if she pursues her

medical studies, could her fortune be put to higher-minded ends?

INTELLECTUAL PATH

6 Self-knowledge

XIII Death – In Tarot, the Grim Reaper is a symbol of new life – the death of the past, "rebirth" as a wiser person, and optimism for the future. As the querent embarks on her new phase, she should be wary of inner obstacles to maturity (the dismembered corpses) such as egotism and over-ambition.

7 Self-control

VI The Lovers – The feminine dichotomy of chaste maiden or seductress points to the querent's choice between the sober study of medicine and the glamour of fashion. But the card is also about reconciling opposites. What do these pursuits have in common? A desire to make others happy?

8 Self-mastery

XII The Hanged Man – The card can suggest indebtedness. The querent might examine her conscience in order to reassure herself that she does not owe her original choice of medicine to a subconscious desire to please her parents, themselves doctors.

EMOTIONAL PATH

9 Compassion

XI Justice – Looking into her own reasons for pursuing medicine, the querent could ask her parents why they made this choice. Was it their heart's desire? If not, it is perhaps not too late to change – and the querent now has the financial means to help them do so.

10 Empathy

III The Empress – The Empress combines feminine nurture and authority – power to transform the lives of others. Does the querent know anyone who needs financial help but may be reluctant to ask? However, like the ideal ruler, she should beware of condescension.

11 Love for all creation

I The Magician – The Magician is another reminder of the power of transformation. Karmically, what goes around, comes around – and vice versa. The querent's windfall is a gift of transformation from the world: in gratitude she might consider a charitable donation.

Tree of Life, Reading 4

The querent is a businesswoman, aged 46, director of a small, non-profit company providing IT training in developing countries. Since founding the company three years ago, she and her fellow director have taken different roles, with the querent handling marketing and personnel and the partner the financial side. The querent needs access to important information on the company's finances but her co-director, whom she trusted as a friend, keeps putting her off with jokey responses.

SPIRITUAL PATH

1 Physical self-awareness

VI The Lovers – The card shows two apparently opposed aspects of the feminine, possibly prompting the querent to assess her business relationship: does the partner's jocularity mask serious differences? Her behaviour may appear at best unprofessional, at worst suspicious – but the male figure suggests the importance of consulting a neutral third party before jumping to conclusions.

2 Awareness of the natural world

XXI The World – The four creatures represent humanity (man), high ideals (eagle), courage (lion) and strength (ox) – qualities that underpin the querent's non-profit organization. Presumably her colleague shares some of these traits – useful to bear in mind while suspicions remain unproven.

3 Awareness of spiritual realities

XIII Death – This card points to spiritual "death" and rebirth,

INTELLECTUAL PATH   SPIRITUAL PATH   EMOTIONAL PATH

8
VII – The *Chariot*

5
XIX – The *Sun*

11
VIII – *Strength*

7
XVII – The *Star*

4
XX – *Judgment*

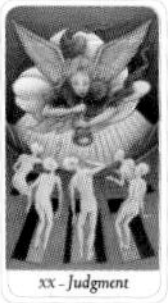

10
II – The *High Priestess*

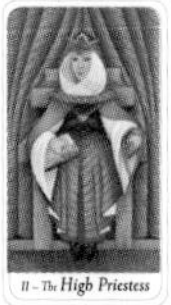

6
XI – *Justice*

3
XIII – *Death*

9
V – The *Hierophant*

2
XXI – The *World*

1
VI – The *Lovers*

231

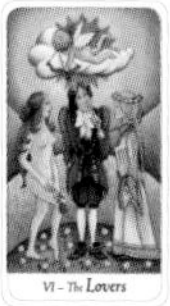

moving away from old, possibly mistaken, attitudes. For her own self-respect – and her legal duty as a director – the querent needs to insist on openness and trust with regard to financial matters.

4 Awareness of inner spirit

XX Judgment – The Last Judgment suggests that the querent might reflect on her own behaviour. Perhaps possessiveness and "empire building" are not entirely one-sided. Has she ever blocked her colleague's attempts to tread on "her" territory, even unwittingly?

5 Awareness of the divine

XIX The Sun – The light of creation shines over the wall and brings harmonious union. With creative thinking, the querent can help convince her fellow director that her request is serious – better than enlisting the company's lawyers, accountants and trustees.

INTELLECTUAL PATH

6 Self-knowledge

XI Justice – The querent is only seeking what is her entitlement as a director – knowledge of her company's finances. But there is another aspect – looking into her own beliefs to assess her real needs and to take stock of her future path, professionally and personally.

7 Self-control

XVII The Star – The Star symbolizes the light of the spirit; and the bird, our higher self. The querent should approach her co-director from the high ground of past trust and friendship, avoiding insinuation of dishonesty while insisting on the changes she wants.

8 Self-mastery

VII The Chariot – The two horses drawing the chariot might seem an apt image of the querent and her colleague. But the horses seem to be pulling in different directions, so perhaps the issue of financial access masks her deeper concerns about the company's direction.

EMOTIONAL PATH

9 Compassion

V The Hierophant – The supplicants before the high priest invite us to examine our moral responsibilities. The querent's business is founded on a desire to help others. She must also think of those closer to home –

her employees and their families. If something feels wrong, it is her moral – and legal – duty to help to put it right.

10 Empathy

II The High Priestess – The all-wise priestess may inspire the querent to approach her colleague in the role of counsellor, encouraging her to be open about any problems – which may have an honest cause.

11 Love for all creation

VIII Strength – The woman clasping the lion's jaws suggests that true strength comes when the spiritual balances the material. In this case, perhaps the reference is to the need to balance the company's idealistic desire to help people with the practical side of business?

233

Tree of Life, Reading 5

The querent is a 41-year-old woman, whose husband left her two years ago. They have a 7-year-old daughter. Her parents had been married for 49 years when the querent's mother died five months ago. She is concerned that her 78-year-old father has recently begun a relationship with his cleaner, 35 years his junior. The querent's younger sister claims that some of their mother's jewelry is missing. The querent is worried because her father seems unwilling to discuss the new relationship.

SPIRITUAL PATH

1 Physical self-awareness

XVII The Star – The naked woman and the outpouring of water under starlight can represent the exposing of unconscious feelings. The querent might begin by clarifying her own emotions: hurt for her late mother's sake; fears for her father's well-being; and perhaps jealousy?

2 Awareness of the natural world

IX The Hermit – The lone spiritual traveller, lighted only by his own lantern, suggests that the querent should follow her own instincts – a surer guide than the opinions of others, who may obscure her judgment with material concerns.

3 Awareness of spiritual realities

VIII Strength – The woman uses gentle strength to tackle the powerful male lion, stilling its roar and bite. This suggests one way in which the querent might approach her father – from a place of love rather than anger or suspicion.

INTELLECTUAL PATH **SPIRITUAL PATH** **EMOTIONAL PATH**

8
XIX – The Sun 

5
0 – The Fool

11
II – The High Priestess

7
X – The Wheel of Fortune 

4
III – The Empress 

10
XVIII – The Moon

6
IV – The Emperor

3
VIII – Strength 

9
XIV – Temperance

2
IX – The Hermit 

1
XVII – The Star 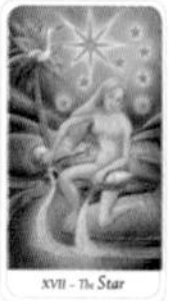

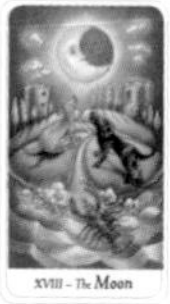

235

4 Awareness of inner spirit

III The Empress – The Empress, whose sceptre and shield represent her command of worldly affairs and powerful protective spirit, may be one who fully knows the extent of the querent's father's loss. Given his likely grief and loneliness, his attachment to another woman, who is willing to care for him, can be seen positively.

5 Awareness of the divine

0 The Fool – The Fool sets out, to be faced with unforeseen challenges. For the querent and her family, the mother's death marks not the end of a journey but a beginning, in which expectations may be confounded. Wisdom lies in understanding the one eternal truth: that everything changes.

INTELLECTUAL PATH

6 Self-knowledge

IV The Emperor – The forceful masculine yang of the Emperor is the counterpart of the Empress' subtler yin dynamism. The emperor's strong will may shade into egotism. The querent could draw on the image to acknowledge self-centred motives in her concerns about her father's partner.

7 Self-control

X The Wheel of Fortune – The turning wheel tells us that we may be certain only of uncertainty. Is the father's new partner a gold digger or a genuinely affectionate companion? The querent should avoid letting her instincts and emotions (the monkey) overwhelm her rational intelligence (the hare).

8 Self-mastery

XIX The Sun – The image of the sun shining on two lovers, divided from the rest of creation by a high wall, could be a striking analogy of the querent's case. It raises the question: has she (with her sister) erected a subjective mental barrier to her father's relationship?

EMOTIONAL PATH

9 Compassion

XIV Temperance – The angel mixes the waters of the spirit/emotion with those of the body/rational mind, once more encouraging the querent to follow a balanced path. This leaves her open to compassion for her bereaved father and the new woman in his life. Perhaps she, too, is simply seeking love and companionship.

10 Empathy

XVIII The Moon – This card can represents the shedding of light on inner feelings. The querent may suspect her father of foolishness, but perhaps his own feelings are tempered by guilt for his late wife's memory. An inability to express such mixed emotions may account for his reluctance to talk.

11 Love for all creation

II The High Priestess – The High Priestess is the inner intuitive guide, our deeper wisdom that overrides egotistical material concerns. Everyone is entitled to happiness, including her father and his partner. Once reassured of the genuineness of their relationship, the querent's wisest course might be to welcome the partner into the family.

Tree of Life, Reading 6

The querent is a single man, aged 31, chief fitness instructor at a leisure centre. Recently he has become close to a junior female colleague, aged 28, helping her to organize a sponsored run for a cystic fibrosis charity – her sister is a sufferer. As the friendship has deepened, she has confided in him, in particular about her separation from a violent boyfriend. One evening the querent confessed that he is in love with her, but she expressed shock, telling him that she did not feel the same way.

SPIRITUAL PATH

1 Physical self-awareness

XXI The World – A card denoting the completion of a journey prompts the querent to wonder whether a good friendship is over. This may not be so, but he has overstepped a boundary. He must re-establish that boundary – and understand why he failed to see it.

2 Awareness of the natural world

IV The Emperor – The Emperor's masculine strength and yang energy are pertinent to the querent, whose livelihood depends on such traits. However, the Emperor must beware of egotism. An excess of self-regard diminishes awareness of others' needs.

3 Awareness of spiritual realities

X The Wheel of Fortune – The monkey symbolizes the impulsiveness that led to the querent's breach with his friend. Wisdom (the sphinx) lies in balancing impulse and instinct

INTELLECTUAL PATH   SPIRITUAL PATH   EMOTIONAL PATH

8

o – The *Fool*

5

XV – The *Devil*

11

XI – *Justice*

7

XVIII – The *Moon*

4

IX – The *Hermit*

10

XIX – The *Sun*

6

VIII – *Strength*

3

X – The *Wheel of Fortune*

9

XX – *Judgment*

2

IV – The *Emperor*

1

XXI – The *World*

239

with mindful presence (the hare): this will enhance his ability to pick up signals.

4 Awareness of inner spirit

IX The Hermit – The Hermit is a reminder that inner truth matters, not external trappings such as physical prowess. Perhaps his friend – whose recent experience of men has been negative – is suspicious of his motives. He may need to convince her of his sincerity.

5 Awareness of the divine

XV The Devil – This is a symbol of challenge, the negative that helps us gain clarity. It warns the querent to reflect on his goals and values, and the chains restraining him. The chained woman reminds him that his friend has problems of her own.

INTELLECTUAL PATH
6 Self-knowledge

VIII Strength – The image of the woman restraining the lion echoes the sense of rejection felt by the querent, who is used to being listened to. His friend's reaction might seem extreme; but perhaps he has taken for granted that what might impress in his public role will also impress in private life.

7 Self-control

XVIII The Moon – This card is linked with the emergence of intuition and wisdom from the waters of the unconscious. The crayfish, connected to the destructive aspect of the feminine, represents his friend's confusion. While remaining available, he may do well to back off for now.

8 Self-mastery

0 The Fool – The card's symbolism relates to moving from ignorance to self-knowledge, a journey in which the Fool forgives his dog's sharp nip when it warns of perils ahead. Once alerted, the Fool can choose a safer route to explore the deeper chasms of the soul.

EMOTIONAL PATH

9 Compassion

XX Judgment – The trumpet-blast is a wake-up call to new life. To resurrect his friendship requires a fresh emotional footing, in which the querent – without damaging his self-esteem – gives space to his friend's needs. Even if the friend withdraws cooperation in the charity run, his role in the event might help demonstrate sincerity.

10 Empathy

XIX The Sun – The garden visible beyond the wall may represent the querent's ideal relationship with a woman – perhaps an unattainable ideal. Could it be that the querent needs to set more realistic relationship goals? Should he write to his friend to express his sincere desire to re-establish their friendship, on the basis of mutual respect?

11 Love for all creation

XI Justice – This figure invites the examination of deeds and motives. Even if the querent cannot fix this relationship, his actions in helping clients to get fitter and in raising money to help others are unlikely to go unnoticed – provided that he is sincere.

Tree of Life, Reading 7

The querent is a single woman, aged 33, with a six-year-old daughter. Since leaving college with a media studies diploma, she has worked in various jobs, including driving for a cab company. Recently she volunteered to work there as a mechanic and enrolled for a degree in mechanical engineering. She would like to work for an engineering company, but thinks her qualifications and employment record will put firms off.

SPIRITUAL PATH

1 Physical self-awareness

X The Wheel of Fortune – The Wheel of Fortune never stops turning, but sometimes twists of fate let us take greater control of our lives. The querent may think her work history looks scrappy, but it led her to discover the work she wants to do. Employers are likely to note the evidence of her determination to make a new start.

2 Awareness of the natural world

XIII Death – The symbol of life's challenges, Death can also represent transition. The querent need not be ashamed of her job history, but present it to potential employers as wide-ranging experience of the real world.

3 Awareness of spiritual realities

XVI The Tower – The tower struck by lightning has been seen as liberation from a negative self-image. The querent must stop seeing herself in terms of what she has not achieved, but rather as one who faces down difficulties.

242

INTELLECTUAL PATH   SPIRITUAL PATH   EMOTIONAL PATH

8
IV – The Emperor

5
XIV – Temperance

11
III – The Empress

7
VII – The Chariot

4
0 – The Fool

10
IX – The Hermit

6
VI – The Lovers

3
XVI – The Tower

9
XVIII – The Moon

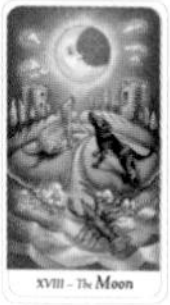

2
XIII – Death

1
X – The Wheel of Fortune

4 Awareness of inner spirit

0 The Fool – The querent tends to view herself as the Fool, setting out on an untried road, enthusiastic but uncertain. She should recall how far she has already travelled. Engineering is new to her, but her awareness of challenges ahead, and her willingness to negotiate them, are signs that she already possesses wisdom and courage.

5 Awareness of the divine

XIV Temperance – This angelic being combines the waters of heaven with those of earth, reminding the querent that life often requires us to balance inner ideals with practical realities. To find this balance is to discover the firm, rich soil in which happiness and fulfilment may flourish.

INTELLECTUAL PATH
6 Self-knowledge

VI The Lovers – On one level, the man who cannot choose between different female archetypes represents the querent's past career uncertainty. But the card is also about uniting different aspects of the self. She should not fudge her resumé – good employers will value her honesty.

7 Self-control

VII The Chariot – The Chariot reflects the next stage of the querent's journey: she has reached the point where old uncertainties (the town) are left behind as she moves forward with confidence. For employers, the fact that she has enrolled for a degree is a clear sign of new commitment.

8 Self-mastery

IV The Emperor – The all-powerful ruler achieves progress and respect through strength, dynamism and creativity rather than force, rigidity and lack of imagination. The shield indicates that the querent need not be defensive about the past – she is in command of her own destiny.

EMOTIONAL PATH

9 Compassion

XVIII The Moon – The powerful feminine energies of the moon are enhanced by the presence of the lactating dog, reminding the querent that for six years she has had a steady career – as a single mother. She should reassure herself that any employer prepared to take her on will be sympathetic to her domestic situation.

10 Empathy

IX The Hermit – The hermit's lantern often symbolizes what is most precious to our well-being. For the querent, this is surely her daughter. If the querent were offered employment away from home, what might the implications be for her daughter's life?

11 Love for all creation

III The Empress – The all-powerful female ruler stares benignly, her gaze steady, her posture open. With a similar attitude, the querent is likely to find that the world will welcome her gifts. Like the Empress, she should bear her blazon lightly, not as a defensive weapon but as a conscious emblem proclaiming her readiness to face and embrace the future.

Seven-card Horseshoe, Reading 8

The querent is a single woman, aged 29, who is at a career impasse. After leaving university with a social science degree she was attracted to journalism and worked as a trainee reporter. She is outgoing, interested in people, with a talent for interviewing and acquiring information, rather than writing. She gave up after a year and since then has held marketing and PR posts. However, she hates office life and thinks she might enjoy counselling or broadcasting, but cannot afford to be a student again. She has a long-term partner and would like a family some day.

1 Past influences

I The Magician – The Magician is the master of transformation, a positive symbol of new beginnings but a skilled deceiver – for good or ill. Like the Magician we possess the power to make problems vanish: either honestly through self-examination, or through self-deception. Habits of self-deception often derive from our parents, and the querent could begin by examining her parents' own attitudes to their careers. Did they do work they loved?

2 Psychological effects

VI The Lovers – This card is often interpreted as representing a dichotomy between different aspects of the feminine – the virgin and the lover; the priestess and the queen; the inner path of (self-) nurture and the outer path of power and status. The querent stands as the central figure, unsure

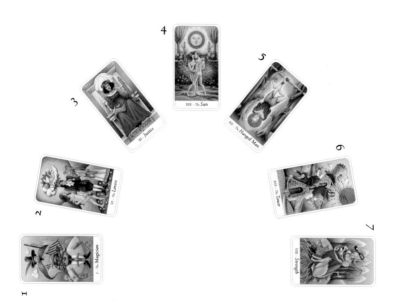

of how to reconcile her outgoing side (radio-presenting, work outside an office) and her more reflective, nurturing side (counselling, motherhood). This makes her unfocused about career options.

3 and 4 Personal qualities that might help with a solution

XI Justice – The figure of justice wields the sword that cuts through the fog of unclarity and uncertainty, and the scales in which truth is weighed against falsehood.

The querent, too, may possess useful tools for progress. She is in a quandary about her career, but that does not mean she is uncertain about all aspects of life. She is aware, for example, of her flair for drawing information out of others. Perhaps she could apply this skill to herself? Putting herself in the roles of reporter and interviewee, or of counsellor and client, she may discover that she holds more answers to her problems than she realizes.

XIX The Sun – A traditional symbol of creativity and enlightenment, the sun banishes the shadows that are cast by mental barriers (the wall) and brings greater light and clarity into our lives. Complementing the introspective aspects of the moon, the sun highlights the querent's extraversion and her ability to deal positively with others. This flair for personal contact may be one key to her future, in terms of discovering work she enjoys and her possible future role of mother.

5 and 6 Personal qualities that might impede a solution

XII The Hanged Man – This card illustrates a medieval penalty for debtors, to make the sufferer change their ways. Does the querent have any habits or attitudes that bar her progress? For example, her aversion to administrative tasks is probably unrealistic, since most work involves paperwork. She assumes that admin is always tedious. However, she should reflect that if she finds work she really enjoys, admin would seem less uncongenial.

XVI The Tower – Open to interpretation, the Tower often represents the fortress-like wall of fixed attitudes with which we may close ourselves to change. Is the querent's vagueness about career options a way of resisting change? Has she wrongly associated her dissatisfaction with failure? Becoming aware of underlying false beliefs may be the bolt of lightning that helps her to break unhelpful patterns and move toward her goal.

7 How you might avoid similar problems in future
VIII Strength – The image of a woman subduing a lion is potent

for the querent, symbolizing the overcoming of her problem. In particular it represents self-mastery – overcoming our most fiercely resistant opponent: ourself. Self-mastery involves looking clearly at our strengths as well as our weaknesses. What makes the querent stand out as an individual and as a potential employee? Active and sociable, she appears to enjoy personal interaction. These skills might be extremely welcome in areas she has not yet considered – perhaps the travel or hospitality businesses.

Seven-card Horseshoe, Reading 9

The querent is a single woman, aged 21, who has worked for four months as a clerical assistant in the marketing department of an electronics manufacturer. It is her first job since gaining a degree in business studies. The manager of her 18-strong team is a woman of 32, recently promoted from within the company. The querent generally finds her straightforward and the workload reasonable. However, she also feels that her manager is sparing in her appreciation and ready to be critical. A few weeks ago the manager invited the women in the team – but not the querent – to her house for drinks. The querent was hurt, but is unsure whether she should bring the matter up with her manager, discuss it with other colleagues or complain to a senior manager.

1 Past influences

II The High Priestess – The High Priestess represents female spiritual power and the acquisition of wisdom. The querent is learning that the informality of student life is different from office life, with its complex web of relationships. The key to wisdom is developing and trusting her intuition and logic.

2 Psychological effects

VIII Strength – This image is symbolically one of the clearest in the Tarot – it concerns the power we possess within to face and overcome challenges. The querent can draw strength from reflecting on what she truly knows. She is upset by the perceived snub; her confidence has suffered and

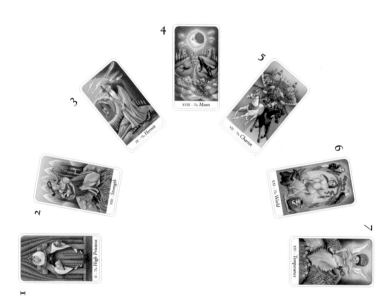

she feels strongly enough to consider taking action. Yet before proceeding she might reflect on whether her manager has ever explicitly expressed any dislike of her or her work. Does the querent know that her work is, on the whole, perfectly good? Knowledge is strength.

3 and 4 Personal qualities that might help with a solution
IX The Hermit – The Hermit reinforces the wisdom of drawing

251

on her own inner resources to shed light on a difficult situation. Since the querent has no conclusive experience of being treated unfairly by the manager, it is probably unlikely that her boss deliberately intended to insult her. How does this understanding alter the querent's perspective?

XVIII The Moon – The Moon is another card traditionally symbolic of (especially female) intuition and hidden mysteries. It might encourage the querent to look more deeply at what lies behind her manager's behaviour, with the empathic eye of a fellow female employee. The manager is fairly new to the job and manufacturing is traditionally male-dominated. Is she under stress? This might explain – if not excuse – her neglecting to praise the work of a junior employee or invite her to a social occasion.

5 and 6 Personal qualities that might impede a solution

VII The Chariot – The Chariot, apparently pulled in two directions, invites us to consider the motives that drive our actions. As indicated by the charioteer's golden crown (wisdom and nobility) and the stars on the brow of each horse (heavenly powers), our higher self is often a wiser guide than feelings of hurt, defensiveness or self-righteousness. By taking the matter further, the querent would lend it a significance that it probably does not deserve. Going to her manager's superior would be, in effect, making an official complaint – too drastic an action in the circumstances. So perhaps the card is warning the querent against emotive overreactions.

XXI The World – This card shows a figure surrounded by the four creatures of Ezekial, symbols representing humanity, spirituality, courage and strength – qualities indicating the completion of our journey to maturity. Pride is not one of these qualities: one aspect of maturity is that sometimes doing nothing is the most courageous path. For example, unless the querent is certain that her manager's snub was deliberate, it would be unreasonable to seek an apology. Restraint may be the steadiest course.

7 How you might avoid similar problems in future

XIV Temperance – The angel of Temperance balances the waters of the conscious and the unconscious, the temporal and the sacred. Associated with fairness, concord and the avoidance of conflict, temperance is a useful quality to cultivate as the querent embarks on a career for which she has good academic training but little practical experience. What the querent can take from her current quandary is that the world of work can turn up tricky situations as we learn to negotiate the untidy boundaries between our working and personal relationships.

Seven-card Horseshoe, Reading 10

The querent is a married woman, aged 42, with two children aged eight and 11. She would like greater contact with her father, who is 82 and frail, but he lives a long way away and finds it difficult to express affection – she tries to call regularly but he is reluctant to talk, rarely asks her about her life, and they often end up arguing. On the other hand, he can be generous, often sending substantial sums on birthdays. When the querent was a child, her businessman father was often absent, working long hours or drinking with friends rather than spending evenings at home. His drinking resulted in marital rows, and after 12 years of marriage the querent's late mother left home when the querent was ten. Her father remarried five years later and the querent finds her stepmother sympathetic, but at times overly protective of her father.

1 Past influences

IX The Hermit – The solitary traveller can symbolize our willingness to undertake new, potentially painful, challenges, drawing solely on inner resources. Like the Hermit, who has abandoned all encumbrances save the guiding light (of wisdom) and the pilgrim's staff, the querent should be aware of past baggage as she seeks a clear way forward.

2 Psychological effects

XXI The World – This card signifies wholeness, reminding us that our entire being and outlook are affected by childhood: a distant

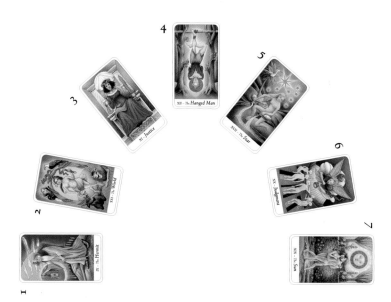

parent, domestic disharmony and divorce can leave deep scars. But the World also represents the ultimate goal of maturity or spiritual wholeness – the querent's willingness to overcome lack of intimacy between herself and her father, symbolized by the physical distance between them.

3 and 4 Personal qualities that might help with a solution

XI Justice – The female figure's sword of wisdom is a widespread

255

symbol of insight that overcomes illusion. With insight comes compassion: she may perceive that her father's gifts are his way of expressing a love he finds difficult to articulate. Why he behaves like this may be rooted in his upbringing. He was a businessman, but was this a self-chosen vocation or a profession his parents pressed on him, leaving him unhappy and frustrated? Heavy drinking and excessive socializing are classic means of avoiding a reality we are reluctant to confront.

XII The Hanged Man – The Hanged Man undergoes a difficult trial, yet his expression is serene and his halo shines with the light of spiritual maturity. One positive consequence of the querent's early experiences may be an acute ability to see beyond appearances in personal relationships, and a determination to forge relationships based on honesty and truth. In seeking to heal the past, the querent can heal the future, both for herself and her children. What has been handed down need not be handed on.

5 and 6 Personal qualities that might impede a solution

XVII The Star – The Star is the classic symbol of guidance, and water denotes the depths of wisdom. The querent actively seeks closer contact with her father through regular phone calls, yet these often end in arguments. Giving way to frustration or anger is counterproductive: one way to avoid this might be to seek the professional guidance of a counsellor, or at least to be guided by her own insight. For example, looking dispassionately (and compassionately) at her father's attitudes, she would realize his difficulty in overcoming such deeply ingrained, lifelong patterns.

XX Judgment – This image of the dead being called to account is a reminder that true personal progress requires self-examination, a commitment to being honest with ourselves. Does the querent have ingrained patterns that may be unhelpful? For example, what she considers her stepmother's over-protectiveness may be rooted in an awareness of her father's vulnerability. After all, the stepmother has lived with her father for longer, and probably knows him better than anyone – which may be an unconscious source of resentment.

7 How you might avoid similar problems in future

XIX The Sun – The regenerative power of the sun, like the union of the female and male figures, denotes the beginnings of growth and renewal and the end of sterility. For the querent, growth means improving a long-term unsatisfactory relationship. This will not be easy, but with compassion and sensitivity, and above all love, she may succeed in overcoming emotional and psychological stumbling-blocks.

Five-card Horseshoe, Reading 11

The querent is a woman aged 37 with a 13-year-old daughter from a previous marriage and a baby son by her 40-year-old husband of one year. A fellow lawyer, he is a loving spouse and father. When the querent first met him, she told him that her first husband had died of cancer four years previously. He told her that he was amicably divorced with a daughter. She has met his ex-wife and daughter and gets on well with them. Recently she Googled her husband and came across an old resumé. To her shock she read that he had a son. Her husband claimed the resumé was not his, but his name is not common and other details fitted. She questioned his brother, who admitted that her husband had been married twice before and had a son by the first marriage. It had been a deeply painful experience and her husband has no contact with his first wife or his son. The querent does not know how to confront her husband. According to the brother, the second ex-wife is also unaware of his first marriage.

1 Past influences

XV The Devil – Tarot reflects an earlier biblical-Kabbalistic tradition that views the Devil as signifying not evil but the confrontation of challenges. As a lawyer, the querent has devoted her life to truth and justice, making it hard for her to accept that her husband has lied to her. Since he too is a lawyer, perhaps she considers him a hypocrite. Yet the querent also knows that the truth is rarely black and white. The flaming

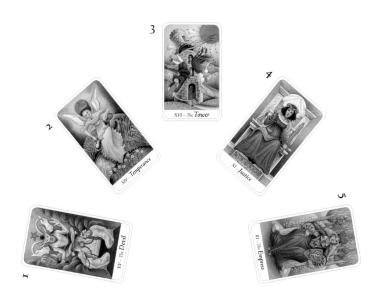

torch reminds us that the Devil is also Lucifer, the light-bearer, defying us to bring light into the darkness of our preconceptions.

2 Psychological effects

XIV Temperance – The waters of heaven and earth mixed by the angel of Temperance point to opposing forces at work within the querent. She feels betrayed and unsure about whether to trust her husband: what else might he have kept from her? She must also wonder why his first wife refuses contact. Is there a history of violence, even though there is no evidence of this and he remains friends with his other ex-wife? He certainly owes the querent an apology, but the essence of temperance is moderation – an approach to the truth that emphasizes the importance of reconciliation.

3 Personal qualities that might help with a solution

XVI The Tower – This image need not be negative. The lightning bolt (shocking new knowledge) that blasts an edifice (relationship with her husband) may remove burdensome layers, leaving the structure more stable. As a lawyer, the querent could discover proof of

the first marriage from official sources. She also has the ability to present evidence to her husband in a way that is neither confrontational nor betrays her brother-in-law's confidence. Perhaps she could begin by subtly exploring with her predecessor the possibility that he ever mistreated her: such reassurance would ease her mind.

4 Personal qualities that might impede a solution

XI Justice – Justice is an apt archetype for a lawyer (such correspondences can occur in the Tarot, though contradictions are equally common). In her work, the querent will often hear different versions of a story, and she may be used to distrusting others' accounts. But she should examine what she knows: that her husband loves her and their baby; that his ex-wife remains his friend; and that the break-up of his first marriage caused him such distress that he cannot speak about it. Perhaps he fears that she will leave him if she learns the truth. While the querent has a right to request clarification of her husband's actions, instinct might lead her support the case for the defence rather than for the prosecution.

5 How you might avoid similar problems in future

III The Empress – This card represents the immediacy of human feelings and emotions. Encountering the Empress' gaze – direct and penetrating, but also wise and compassionate – we are invited to question the depth of understanding with which we engage with others. As a loving mother, how would the querent feel if she was denied contact with her children? The pain of loss would be akin to the grief she presumably felt at the death of her first husband. An empathetic approach, demonstrating to her husband that she understands what he may be feeling, probably offers the best chance of helping him to open up to her – and moving the relationship to a place of honesty and trust.

Celtic Cross, Reading 12

The querent is a full-time mother, aged 44. Her husband works long hours in the HR department of a large company. Their children, aged five and nine, are both at school and the querent has been considering returning to work. She trained in occupational therapy, but after ten years feels she will be unable to find work. Bored, she has recently become close friends with a neighbour, the father of two college-aged children and the husband of a good friend. He works from home and the querent has taken to dropping in for coffee. She realizes she may have feelings for him and thinks they may be returned. She is unsure whether to raise the matter for fear of losing a friend and of deceiving her husband, whom she loves. Her own mother left home for another man.

Card chosen to represent the situation

VI The Lovers – The Lovers stand for two aspects of femininity: the practical, ordered side (the querent's role of mother and homemaker, as well as her therapeutic training); and the more creative, uninhibited side, less bound by "duty". The issue focuses on how the querent reconciles these aspects while attaining personal fulfilment.

1 General influences affecting the question

IV The Emperor – In one sense the Emperor represents the dominant male figure in the querent's life – husband or potential lover. But on a more complex level he suggests

4

XI – *Justice*

5

VIII – *Strength*

I

2

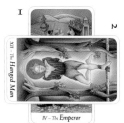

XII – *The* Hanged Man

IV – *The* **Emperor**

6

VII – *The* **Chariot**

3

XVIII – *The* **Moon**

personal sovereignty – free will and what we do with it. The wise Emperor seeks to be honest about the motives and consequences of actions that will affect others. Is the querent's attraction to her friend's husband purely sexual? Or does he represent freedom – creative, independent, free from childcare?

2 Obstacles in the way

XII The Hanged Man – This image resonates with the querent's sense of being trapped. Added to the guilt occasioned by her feelings toward another man is perhaps the sense that she contributes little financially to family income. But she must not assume that her situation is hopeless. The Hanged Man is also a symbol of transition: he is putting the past behind

him and his serenity points to a positive future.

3 Inner strengths

XVIII The Moon – The moon is associated with the mysterious depths of the unconscious – from which emerges a crayfish that hints at a (self-) destructive aspect. For the querent, clear relationship boundaries may be blurred by a deep conviction that she is fated to repeat her mother's behaviour. Such patterns can arise when we are unfocused. It might help if the querent could focus energy on finding fulfilling work: might a therapy refresher course help?

4 Past experiences

XI Justice – Justice means doing right, but defining "right" involves dispassionate discernment. The querent might reflect on the effect of her own mother's departure. Would her personal freedom be worth the hurt and sacrifices? Such reflections may put her feelings into perspective. Another of her skills, also from her therapy training, may be an ability to talk to people to find out their needs. Perhaps she could work with her husband to enhance their relationship without raising alarms. This might bring them closer together, enabling her to deal distantly with the friend.

5 Hopes and aspirations

VIII Strength – This card is about self-mastery – overcoming forces that hold us back. The querent should look closely at her idea that she has been out of work for too long. Perhaps it would not be so difficult to do some top-up training; and researching and following a suitable course might give her focus and confidence.

6 Future experiences

VII The Chariot – This card suggests "progress" – it is the point when the Fool begins to move from ignorance to clarity. Like the charioteer whose horses seemingly pull at cross purposes, the querent has become aware of the many forces that draw us, sometimes in conflicting directions. To keep partner, family, friendships and work in balance can be difficult. Balance will only be achieved if we allow time and space for personal fulfilment – this helps us to keep a steady hand on the chariot of destiny.

Celtic Cross, Reading 13

The querent is a girl, aged 17, who wants to study economics. But her exam grades were poor, so she is taking a year out for re-sits. She blames her grades on the stress of coping with her alcoholic mother while revising. Her mother's drinking has driven the querent's father to leave home, taking her younger sister. He pays the mortgage on the family home and the rent on a small apartment near by. The querent chose to stay with her mother, hoping the drinking might ease, but recently her mother was suspended from her job and her problems worsened. First thing in the morning she is fine, but she soon starts on her first glass of wine of the day. The querent regularly suffers hurtful abuse. Whenever she tries to discuss the situation with her mother, the woman becomes aggressive.

Card chosen to represent the situation

XVI The Tower – This symbolizes the destructive effects of her mother's behaviour. It can also represent spiritual loss, perhaps the feeling that she has lost her mother and family stability. It also reminds us that change is inevitable and a crisis can mean positive renewal.

1 General influences affecting the question

XV The Devil – The Devil can represent the Shadow archetype, which drives negative behaviour. Unless acknowledged, the Shadow will remain a potent force for (self-)destructive actions. This refers not only to the central issue of her mother's alcoholism but also to her

4

XIV – *Temperance*

5

V – *The* **Hierophant**

1

2

III – *The Empress*

XV – *The* **Devil**

6

XIII – *Death*

3

X – *The* **Wheel** *of* **Fortune**

own unacknowledged feelings, such as anger at the disruption to her own life. Perhaps she unconsciously blames herself.

2 Obstacles in the way

III The Empress – The Empress, often a positive force, can become overbearing and self-centred, with the power to withdraw her bounty as well as to grant it. One effect of the mother's illness is to turn her role from mother to one in which she, not her children, needs most care. The illness has also put the querent's family under financial pressure. This may be an issue when seeking professional help.

3 Inner strengths

X The Wheel of Fortune – The Wheel of Fortune hints at the mental and spiritual tools that help us with life's changes. The querent is poised between childhood and independence. The role-reversal by which she cares for her mother, rather than vice versa, is a steep, confusing learning curve. She can draw on the inner resources that led her to remain with her mother initially. She could suggest her father returns home, which would reduce her burden and make practical help easier.

4 Past experiences

XIV Temperance – The angel of Temperance embodies the ancient Greek maxim, "moderation in all things". Temperance also refers to abstaining from alcohol. Is it possible for the mother to return to her sobriety of only a few years ago? If she remains in denial to her immediate family, perhaps a relative could come and visit in the mornings, when the querent is more approachable, and exert a moderating influence based on family ties and rooted in past shared happiness.

5 Hopes and aspirations

V The Hierophant – A hierophant is a holy teacher who guides seekers to spiritual fulfilment. For the querent, "spiritual" includes development as an autonomous adult. She is on the verge of leaving home, but perhaps feels guilt at "abandoning" her mother. Is she certain that this played no part in her exam results and her decision to remain at home? It may even be reflected in her decision to stay with her mother when her father and sister left. But she must recognize that her love for her mother must not be confused with total responsibility for her. Her mother alone can put an end to the alcohol abuse, and it is the father who must take the lead in seeking help for her.

6 Future experiences

XIII Death – Something needs to perish for renewal to take place. Perhaps what needs to be rejected is the idea of sacrificial devotion. If she cannot study effectively at home, perhaps she must make arrangements to study elsewhere. She needs to live her own life, and see friends when she can. A degree of independence will help her to deal with her family stresses.

Celtic Cross, Reading 14

The querent is a married man, aged 37, separated from his wife for two years. She lives with their son, aged 11, in the home they jointly own, although they share childcare. The querent initiated the split, claiming they had drifted apart because of the wife's workload. No third party was involved, but the split was acrimonious. For the last year he has been dating another woman. His wife also had a brief affair. The querent now wants a divorce so he can marry his new partner and he wishes to sell the home. But the wife refuses those terms. When they were together she was the main earner and paid for him to train as a psychotherapist. After angry calls and emails, his wife's lawyer stated that all communication must now be in writing. She also wants the custody agreement to be formalized, with her husband allowed weekend access only.

Card chosen to represent the situation

Three of Pentacles – Three represents the querent, his wife and their son. The Three of Pentacles can denote the merit we carry into future lives on earth; it also connotes the complexity of human existence and the benefit of following our instinct.

1 General influences affecting the question

Two of Wands – Two represents separation. Here the potential for conflict is emphasized by the wands, which may be weapons or staffs. The querent might reflect that while conflict can be constructive, it depends

4

o – The *Fool*

5

King of Cups

1

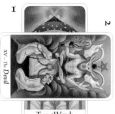

XV – The *Devil*

Two of Wands

2

6

VI – The *Lovers*

3

Queen of Wands

271

whether our motives are positive or negative.

2 Obstacles in the way

XV The Devil – This card represents life's challenges – perhaps the chained figures are suffering humans unable to break their bonds. As part of a divorce settlement, the querent wishes to sell their house, so that he can receive his share; she, for her part, feels that her financial contribution to the marriage, and to his career, has been repaid only with abandonment. She feels she owes him nothing and it is hardly surprising that his inflexible response to her refusal has led to worsening relations. How would things be if he had not made this demand? What if he dropped it?

3 Inner strengths

Queen of Wands – This queen symbolizes the wife's maternal side. The unicorn and the sprouting wands point to her ability to use anger positively. In his psychotherapy training the querent learned how to listen non-judgmentally. If he could see the relationship from his wife's viewpoint, perhaps a way forward might emerge.

4 Past experiences

0 The Fool – The Fool represents ourselves on life's journey. The chasm may suggest the rift that has opened in a marriage, the dog some kind of lingering fidelity – perhaps to honourable action. Our wisdom derives from dealings with others. Communication has broken down totally. In moving forward, this seems to be the primary issue for the querent, not least for their son's sake. The querent might reflect on the early days of their marriage. How did they communicate? When did they stop talking? Such questions may help him to persuade his wife to reopen communication.

5 Hopes and aspirations

King of Cups – This king bears the trident of Neptune or Poseidon, the stormy god of the sea, and his horse rears, symbolizing the impulsive aspect of the ruler, whose bursts of transforming energy may manifest as enthusiasm or aggression. Perhaps the querent's present happy relationship has overridden sensitivity toward his wife. The king's impulsiveness may clash with his paternal side, so the querent should examine how his attention to his new partner impacts upon his son.

6 Future experiences

VI The Lovers – The figures stand for the querent and the two women. They might induce the querent to examine his relationships with women in general. He appears bewildered by his wife's behaviour, and unable to see her hurt. Her demands reflect deep anger over his decision to leave her after she had worked so hard for the family. For relations with his wife to improve, the querent might acknowledge her feelings and take on responsibility for them. What can he do to ease the discomforts felt by all?

Celtic Cross, Reading 15

The querent, a married woman aged 27, is an assistant manager in the finance department of an energy company, where she began working as accounts trainee six years ago. She recently applied for the post of assistant finance director. The director has invited her for interview and implied that she will be successful. She is ambitious and would love the challenges that this senior post would bring. However, she has just learned that she is five weeks pregnant. The pregnancy was planned and her husband, a freelance IT consultant, has agreed to give up his job for a period to care for the child. She is concerned that her employers would be displeased if she were to land the job and then announce her need for maternity leave. On the other hand, she worries that she may adversely affect her chances of promotion if she now tells her superiors, who are all men, that she is pregnant.

Card chosen to represent the situation

VIII Strength – This is a delicate and difficult issue that has considerable implications for the querent's future. The Strength card represents her ability to confront and overcome challenges. She is used to dealing with the tests and trials that arise in her career, and she should take courage that these skills will serve her well as she considers her current dilemma.

1 General influences affecting the question

XII The Hanged Man – The card highlights the basic fear that lies at

V – The Hierophant

o – The Fool

Princess of Cups

XII – The Hanged Man

Four of Swords

Ten of Cups

the heart of the querent's problem: that she will be penalized for being pregnant. Perhaps pregnancy is having an effect on her physically and mentally, making it difficult to apply cold logic. Certainly, in a metaphorical sense, it is turning her life upside down. The Hanged Man, however, has an expression of serenity, suggesting the positive side of her dilemma: at least she is healthy and fertile, and she feels good about future motherhood. She might begin by reflecting that she has done nothing wrong and her situation is hardly unique.

2 Obstacles in the way

Princess of Cups – The dolphin is a symbol of childbirth, owing to the similarity of the Greek *delphis* (dolphin) and *delphys* (womb),

and this card resonates with other aspects of the problem. In some Tarot decks, the princesses are depicted as pages or knaves (jacks), and hence may have tricksterish qualities – especially an inclination for concealment. However, the Princess of Cups counters this with gentleness, creativity and generosity, while the Cups court cards in general are linked with domesticity and reflection. The querent's decision has implications for her family's finances, and she is inclined to conceal her pregnancy because her promotion would bring additional income. The promotion would be doubly welcome because the querent's husband has agreed to give up work to be the principal carer after her maternity leave. However, this aspect of the situation will surely speak in her favour, because it shows her long-term commitment to working for her employer.

3 Inner strengths

Ten of Cups – The culmination of the numbered cards, the tens represent completion and achievement. The Ten of Cups, in particular, is often understood as representing our own contribution to the key aspects of our lives – what we put into career, family, relationships. The querent is accustomed to giving a great deal. She is clearly devoted to her work, and she is supported in this by her husband. As far as relationships are concerned, the most relevant is that with her employers. Everything suggests that her superiors regard her contribution highly. She might reflect on which possible course would be more likely to build on a relationship that surely must be founded partly on respect for her honesty and integrity.

4 Past experiences

V The Hierophant – The powerful male figure of the Hierophant brings up one aspect of the querent's difficulty – the fact that her company is largely male, and that therefore her colleagues may not be sympathetic. Yet there is no evidence that such a response is likely. Gender bias seems to have by no mean hindered her career so far – given her rapid promotion from accounts junior to the highly responsible senior role of assistant finance director. If her superiors listen to what she has to say in company matters, they are likely also to take her seriously when she wishes to discuss more personal matters.

5 Hopes and aspirations

0 The Fool – The Fool is the traveller through life who, as he acquires wisdom, grows aware of potential pitfalls. The querent's apprehension about upsetting her position at work arises from her desire to establish a stable and successful career–family set-up, a tricky balancing act that many working parents have to contend with. She is excited at the prospects that lie ahead in her professional career. At the same time she is committed to having a family. The arrangement with her husband indicates her desire to ensure that even if she herself will not be a full-time mother, the child will be in the constant care of a parent rather than a childminder or nursery. Yet she is unsure whether her male employers will endeavour, with equal dedication, to accommodate her pregnancy. Expressing her commitment to making the balance work would be one useful way of countering any objections.

6 Future experiences

Four of Swords – The sword is a symbol of equity and protection, while the number four (like the square) denotes security and stability. In most Western countries, there are laws to protect male and female workers from unfair treatment. For example, workers in the US are not legally obliged to tell employers that they are pregnant, while in Europe they are obliged to inform their employers only at 15 weeks. This is understandable, because many pregnancies do not proceed beyond the early stages. However, if the querent cannot legally be penalized for saying nothing at this stage, she may find that aspects of the pregnancy (such as regular bouts of morning sickness) may adversely affect her work in ways that would be difficult to explain away without being positively dishonest. The sword is also a symbol of truth, and perhaps it is time to repay the confidence invested in her by her superiors by seeking now to confide in them in return. She might find it easier to talk privately with just one person, such as her current immediate superior – assuming she has a good working and personal relationship with him. She may be surprised at the sympathetic response she receives, and she is likely to feel better for opening up to someone. At any rate, she will at least gain some idea of how her pregnancy is likely to be received by other senior colleagues.

Further Reading

Banzhaf, Hajo and Theler, Brigitte, *Tarot and the Journey of the Hero*, Samuel Weiser Inc., Maine, 2000

Bias, Clifford, *Qabalah, Tarot and the Western Mystery Traditions: The 22 Connecting Paths on the Tree of Life*, Samuel Weiser Inc., Maine, 1997

Eason, Cassandra, *Complete Guide to the Tarot*, The Crossing Press Inc., California, 2000; Judy Piatkus, London, 1999

Echols, Signe E., Mueller, Robert, and Thomson, Sandra A., *Spiritual Tarot: Seventy-Eight Paths to Personal Development*, Avon Books, New York, 1996

Fontana, David, *The Truth-Seeker's Tarot*, Duncan Baird Publishers, London, 2008*

Greer, Mary K. and Little, Tom, *Understanding the Tarot Court*, Llewellyn Publications, Minnesota, 2004

Hamaker-Zondag, Karen, *Tarot as a Way of Life: A Jungian Approach to the Tarot*, Samuel Weiser Inc., Maine, 1997

Kaplan, Stuart R., *The Encyclopedia of Tarot, 4 Volume Set*, U.S. Games Systems Inc., New York, 2006

Knight, Gareth, *The Magical World of the Tarot: Fourfold Mirror of the Universe*, Samuel Weiser Inc., Maine, 1996

Nichols, Sallie, *Jung and Tarot: An Archetypal Journey*, Samuel Weiser Inc., Maine, 1996

Place, Robert M., *The Tarot: History, Symbolism and Divination*, Jeremy P. Tarcher/Penguin Group Inc., New York, 2005

* This is a combined book and deck. The deck uses the card designs in *The Essential Guide to the Tarot*.

Index